Working Text

Working Text

X-Word Grammar and Writing Activities for Students

Sue Livingston

Gallaudet University Press
Washington, DC

Gallaudet University Press
Washington, DC 20002
http://gupress.gallaudet.edu

This workbook is based on the work of Linda Ann Kunz and Laurie Gluck 2000.

Printed in the United States of America

16 15 14 13 12 11 10   1 2 3 4 5 6

ISBN 1-56368-468-3, 978-1-56368-468-5

∞ The paper used in this publication meets the minimum requirements of American National Standard for Information Sciences—Permanence of Paper for Printed Library Materials, ANSI Z39.48-1984.

Contents

SECTION 3

Sentence Patterns and Editing Practice

Appendices

To the Student

Several years ago, I met a teacher at LaGuardia Community College named Linda Ann Kunz. At the time I met Linda, I had been teaching reading and writing to Deaf students at LaGuardia for about sixteen years, and I had never been satisfied with the way I taught grammar to help students improve their writing. Linda taught hearing students who speak languages other than English how to write better and used a system of teaching called "X-Word Grammar," which I had never heard of before. But after studying the system, I felt that X-Word Grammar would be a great help to Deaf students.

In this book, you will learn what X-words are, how they show where the subject of a sentence is, how they show time, and how they can tell you if the subject of your sentence is about one person or thing or two or many people and things. You will learn how X-words match with verbs, and how three of them—and only three of them—"hide" inside verbs. You will also learn seven sentence patterns and see how nouns "live inside boxes" and how these boxes can also show one or many and even be replaced by words we will learn are called referents. You will learn these elements of X-Word Grammar in mini-lessons that will be fun for you. (Yes, I am using fun and grammar in the same sentence!)

Step by step, once you learn your lessons, you will put on your grammatical glasses and study how what you learned is used in the kinds of writing your teacher expects you to do. This is a very important part of learning grammar. Your teacher will give you lots of practice reading grammatically before she asks you to do the next task . . . which is to correct mistakes in your own writing. Don't worry, your teacher will use special symbols to help you find these errors, and she or he will expect you to work on correctness only after both of you are satisfied with the ideas that you have written in your required writing.

I would say that about seventy-five deaf college students have studied X-Word Grammar with me over the past eight years. They all have asked me the same thing: "Why didn't I learn this in high school?" I am pretty sure that means they benefited from learning it, as I think you will too. Remember: do your work diligently and study for your quizzes. When you work in teams with your classmates, if you think your answer is correct, argue for it. Learn the grammatical reasons why you are sure you are right. Say things like, "That main verb has a DO X-word hiding inside." Most important, remember that you can become better at grammar on your own by reading with your grammatical glasses on, noting how the grammatical chunks of language you study with your teacher function in whatever it is that you are reading. Soon you will be able to analyze anything that you read grammatically, and that will help you a lot in your writing.

Section 1

• Discovering X-Words and Subjects
• How X-Words Show Time
• How X-Words Match with Subjects
• Editing Practice

Key teaching points:

X-words are powerful.

They show time and how many in the subject.

They have two faces.

ACTIVITY 1 **Using X-Words: 20 Yes/No Questions**

Think of 20 questions that you can answer "yes" or "no" to (for example, "Is it small?") to discover what your teacher has in a bag and write them below. Start each question with a different word from the chart in activity 2, which you will fill in with your teacher. These words are called X-WORDS!

1. Is it small? ______ ______
2. Would I eat it? ______ ______
3. ______ ______
4. ______ ______
5. ______ ______
6. ______ ______
7. ______ ______
8. ______ ______
9. ______ ______
10. ______ ______
11. ______ ______
12. ______ ______
13. ______ ______
14. ______ ______
15. ______ ______
16. ______ ______
17. ______ ______
18. ______ ______
19. ______ ______
20. ______ ______

ACTIVITY 2 Make an X-Word Chart

Fill in the chart below with your teacher, and you will have all 20 X-words!

The DO Family	**Do**	______	______		
The HAVE Family	**Have**	______	______		
The BE Family	**Is**	______	______	______	______
The MODAL Family	**Will**	______	______	______	______
	______	______	______	______	

ACTIVITY 3 X-Words and Subjects: Statements

After discovering what was in the bag, change your questions to statements only if they are true. This means that each X-word will move to the right of the subject, and you will remove the question mark and replace it with a period. When you have finished, put an X on top of each X-word and draw a box around each subject.

1. It is small.
2.
3.
4.
5.
6.
7.
8.
9.
10.
11.
12.
13.
14.
15.
16.
17.
18.
19.
20.

ACTIVITY 4 X-Words and *Not* and *n't*: Negative Statements

Now change the remaining questions (the ones you answered "no" to) to *negative statements*. This means that you will need to add the word *not* or the letters *n't* to each X-word. When you have finished, put an X on top of each X-word and draw a box around each subject.

1. ______________________________

2. I would not eat it. I wouldn't eat it.

3. ______________________________

4. ______________________________

5. ______________________________

6. ______________________________

7. ______________________________

8. ______________________________

9. ______________________________

10. ______________________________

11. ______________________________

12. ______________________________

13. ______________________________

14. ______________________________

15. ______________________________

16. ______________________________

17. ______________________________

18. ______________________________

19. ______________________________

20. ______________________________

ACTIVITY 5 Finding X-Words and Subjects: Making Yes/No Questions #1

Mark each X-word in the passage below and draw a box around its subject. There are 17 X-words for you to find. (*Hint*: Don't miss X-words that are shortened to *contractions* like *it's* for *it is*.) Words that look like X-words after the word *to* (e.g., *do* in *to* do) are not X-words. When you are finished, change sentences 1–5 into yes/no questions. Use your own paper for that.

From **"Pencils"** in ***Wayside School Is Falling Down***
by Louis Sachar, pp. 66–67

Jason borrowed a pencil from Allison. When he gave it back to her, [it] **X** was full of teeth marks.

Allison held the pencil by its point. "Yuck!" she said. "You chewed on it."

Jason felt awful. **1.** [It] **X** is very embarrassing to borrow somebody's pencil and then chew on it. "Sorry," he said. "I didn't mean to chew it on purpose."

"You can keep it," said Allison. She dropped the pencil on Jason's desk, then raised her hand. "Mrs. Jewls, can I go to the bathroom? I must wash my hands. Jason slobbered all over my pencil."

Everybody laughed.

Jason turned red. "I'm sorry, Allison," he said. **2.** "It's a disgusting habit. I just can't help it." . . .

3. Jason was so mad at himself. He broke the chewed up pencil to bits.

4. That wasn't a smart thing to do.

"Everybody take out a pencil and a piece of paper," said Mrs. Jewls. "It's time for our spelling test."

Jason slapped himself on the forehead. "I'm so stupid!" he thought. "Rondi, may I borrow a pencil, please?" he asked.

Rondi made a face. **5.** "All my pencils are new. How do I know you won't eat them?"

ACTIVITY 6 Finding X-Words and Subjects: Making Yes/No Questions #2

Mark each X-word in the passage below and draw a box around its subject. There are 21 X-words for you to find. (*Hint*: Don't miss X-words that are shortened to contractions like *he'd* for *he had*.) When you are finished, change sentences 1–5 into yes/no questions. Use your own paper for that. (*Hint*: If a sentence has two X-words, only the first X-word gets moved.)

From ***A Letter to Mrs. Roosevelt***
by C. Coco De Young, pp. 1–2

I never used to pay much attention to the dark. Well, except for the nights when I sat on our front porch swing, counting the stars and waiting. [I] **X** would find a patch of stars caught between the rooftops across the street and swing and count, and count and wait.

One night my best friend's mother called to me from her porch next door, "Margo, go inside. It's raining. There are no stars for you to count."

"Thank you, Mrs. Meglio, but I can still see the stars from last night," I called back. I didn't tell her that my eyes were closed tight and I was trying to remember them.

1. Nighttime was my friend back then, keeping me company while I waited for the trolley car to bring Mama and Papa home. I could hear the clatter as it crossed over the First Street Bridge and turned right onto Maple Avenue. **2.** Papa would climb down the steps, then hold out his hand to Mama. **3.** I could tell right then if Charlie's day had been all right.

4. Charlie had been kicked in the knee when he'd tried to break up a fight between two boys during a game of kickball. He'd convinced Mama and Papa that it was an accident, but I was not sure. **5.** I can remember hearing Charlie groan during the night. When the doctor visited, he told Papa to get Charlie to the hospital immediately.

I was seven. The hospital rules posted in the front lobby said I was too young to visit my brother. So, I stayed home, although Sister Cecilia did sneak me up to the third-floor children's ward to see Charlie one time.

ACTIVITY 7 X-Words and Time #1

In "Pencils" (activity 5) some X-words are used to talk about BEFORE time and some X-words are used to talk about NOW time. Go back and write B over the X-words that talk about BEFORE time and N over the X-words that talk about NOW time. (See Appendix A for a complete list of BEFORE and NOW X-words to help you.) Here is an example.

From **"Pencils"** in ***Wayside School is Falling Down***
by Louis Sachar, pp. 66–67

X-B

Jason borrowed a pencil from Allison. When he gave it back to her, it was full of teeth marks.

Allison held the pencil by its point. "Yuck!" she said. "You chewed on it."

X-N

Jason felt awful. It is very embarrassing to borrow somebody's pencil and then chew on it.

"Sorry," he said. "I didn't mean to chew it on purpose."

"You can keep it," said Allison. She dropped the pencil on Jason's desk, then raised her hand.

"Mrs. Jewls, can I go to the bathroom? I must wash my hands. Jason slobbered all over my pencil."

Everybody laughed.

Jason turned red. "I'm sorry, Allison," he said. "It's a disgusting habit. I just can't help it." . . .

Jason was so mad at himself. He broke the chewed up pencil to bits.

That wasn't a smart thing to do.

"Everybody take out a pencil and a piece of paper," said Mrs. Jewls. "It's time for our spelling test."

Jason slapped himself on the forehead. "I'm so stupid!" he thought. "Rondi, may I borrow a pencil, please?" he asked.

Rondi made a face. "All my pencils are new. How do I know you won't eat them?"

ACTIVITY 8 X-Words and Time #2

In *A Letter to Mrs. Roosevelt* (activity 6) some X-words are used to talk about BEFORE time and some X-words are used to talk about NOW time. Go back and write B over the X-words that talk about BEFORE time and N over the X-words that talk about NOW time. (See Appendix A for a complete list of BEFORE and NOW X-words to help you.) Here is an example.

From ***A Letter to Mrs. Roosevelt***
by C. Coco De Young, pp. 1–2

I never used to pay much attention to the dark. Well, except for the nights when I sat on our front

X-B
porch swing, counting the stars and waiting. I would find a patch of stars caught between the rooftops across the street and swing and count, and count and wait.

One night my best friend's mother called to me from her porch next door, "Margo, go inside.

X-N **X-N**
It's raining. There are no stars for you to count."

"Thank you, Mrs. Meglio, but I can still see the stars from last night," I called back. I didn't tell her that my eyes were closed tight and I was trying to remember them.

Nighttime was my friend back then, keeping me company while I waited for the trolley car to bring Mama and Papa home. I could hear the clatter as it crossed over the First Street Bridge and turned right onto Maple Avenue. Papa would climb down the steps, then hold out his hand to Mama. I could tell right then if Charlie's day had been all right.

Charlie had been kicked in the knee when he'd tried to break up a fight between two boys during a game of kickball. He'd convinced Mama and Papa that it was an accident, but I was not sure. I can remember hearing Charlie groan during the night. When the doctor visited, he told Papa to get Charlie to the hospital immediately.

I was seven. The hospital rules posted in the front lobby said I was too young to visit my brother. So, I stayed home, although Sister Cecilia did sneak me up to the third-floor children's ward to see Charlie one time.

ACTIVITY 9 X-Words and Time #3

Mark each X-word in the passage below and draw a box around its subject. There are 33 X-words for you to find. Write B over the X-words that talk about BEFORE time and N over the X-words that talk about NOW time. (*Do* in *to do* is not an X-word.)

"My Parents"

X-N
Are [you] proud of your parents? I'm proud of mine. Do you enjoy being with them? I do enjoy being with mine. Let me tell you a little bit about them.

My mother is a terrific cook. She has been cooking delicious (and healthy!) meals for us for as long as I have been old enough to eat them. She doesn't spend a lot of time preparing meals, though, because all her recipes are simple and quick. One recipe for lasagna was selected as the best in a contest she entered a few years ago. Needless to say, we were all thrilled when she brought home the blue ribbon. It was so amazing!

My father is an expert carpenter. He has been building cabinets, desks, closets and even beds since he was a young man. His closets are filled with shelves for sweaters and shoes, and when other people see them, they are impressed with his skill. He doesn't build things for other people – just for us. That is why whatever he makes, we really treasure and consider special.

My mother and father are also a lot of fun to be with. They have traveled to many different countries, and they are knowledgeable about different customs. Their stories are interesting to hear. They don't eat out often (and you probably know why), but they do like to go to museums. Our local museum doesn't charge admission on Tuesday evenings, so every Tuesday they eat an early dinner and leave the house by 6:30 PM. Those Tuesday evenings are their favorite nights! When they come home, they are filled with excitement about paintings that inspired them. Now, do I always enjoy being with my parents? I don't when they are talking to me about chores and homework that I need to do. But, aside from those times, they're pretty cool parents. P.S. I was happy to share them with you!

ACTIVITY 10 Subject and X-Word Match-Ups #1

On the lines below each set of X-words, write the subjects from "My Parents" (activity 9) that match-up with the X-words. Do not use the subject *I* and do not repeat subjects.

Is Was Has Does

My mother ______ ______ ______

______ ______ ______

______

Are Were Have Do

You ______ ______

______ ______ ______

______ ______

What letter does the first group of X-words end with? ______

Can that letter mean *singular* or 1 subject? Yes! *You* will always match with 2 or many.

Which family of X-words is missing on this page? Check Appendix B to see if you can figure this out, and the reason for it.

______

______

ACTIVITY 11 **Subject and X-Word Match-Ups #2**

Which is the only subject from "My Parents" (activity 9) that matches with all of these X-words?

DO WAS AM HAVE

ACTIVITY 12 **X-Words and Time #4**

Mark each X-word in the passage below and draw a box around its subject. There are 35 X-words for you to find. Write B over the X-words that talk about BEFORE time and N over the X-words that talk about NOW time.

"On the Evening of September 11th, 2001"

X-N

September 11, 2001 is a day never to be forgotten. People are still shaking their heads in disbelief. There are many thoughts that they share. We are hearing that many teachers were very brave. They were frightened but knew their students were depending on them. They are to be applauded because not one student was injured. All were escorted to safety.

There is one man who has done a terrific job of making people feel safe. He is Mayor Giuliani. He and his workers were trapped in a building and escaped through a side door. He was pictured running away from the falling debris. Many New Yorkers have said they have never seen the Mayor function so beautifully. He was in charge right from the first few moments. He and his staff are to be congratulated because they have made us all proud.

Of course the firemen and police officers are heroes as well. Many have lost their lives trying to rescue others. Those at Ground Zero do not want to stop looking for possible survivors. They don't believe anyone is alive, but they are determined to keep looking. The Police Commissioner has said that he was thrilled that there was very little looting, but looting was not on most people's minds.

What happens now? We need to be patient. President Bush has been placed in a very difficult situation. The World Trade Center tragedy is the worst attack directly on America that we have ever experienced. He and the members of his cabinet do know that. We are going to need to wait and allow them time to work on a response.

ACTIVITY 13 Subject and X-Word Match-Ups #3

On the lines below each set of X-words, write the subjects from "On the Evening of September 11th, 2001" (activity 12) that match-up with the X-words. Do not repeat subjects.

Is Was Has Does

September 11, 2001 ______ ______ ______

______ ______ ______

______ ______

______

Are Were Have Do

People ______ ______ ______ ______

______ ______ ______

______ ______

______ ______

______

______

ACTIVITY 14 **Subject and X-Word Match-Ups #4**

In "My Parents" (activity 9) some X-words are used to talk about 1 and some X-words are used to talk about 2 or many. Go back and write a 1 over the X-words that talk about 1 subject and a 2 over the X-words that talk about two or more subjects. Do not label the subject *I* for 1 or 2. (See Appendix B for a complete list of X-words that show 1 or 2 or many to help you.) Here is an example.

X-N2 **X-N** **X-N2** **X-N**

Are you proud of your parents? I'm proud of mine. Do you enjoy being with them? I do enjoy being with mine. Let me tell you a little bit about them.

X-N1

My mother is a terrific cook. She has been cooking delicious (and healthy!) meals for us for as long as I have been old enough to eat them. She doesn't spend a lot of time preparing meals, though, because all her recipes are simple and quick. One recipe for lasagna was selected as the best in a contest she entered a few years ago. Needless to say, we were all thrilled when she brought home the blue ribbon. It was so amazing!

My father is an expert carpenter. He has been building cabinets, desks, closets and even beds since he was a young man. His closets are filled with shelves for sweaters and shoes, and when other people see them, they are impressed with his skill. He doesn't build things for other people – just for us. That is why whatever he makes, we really treasure and consider special.

My mother and father are also a lot of fun to be with. They have traveled to many different countries, and they are knowledgeable about different customs. Their stories are interesting to hear. They don't eat out often (and you probably know why), but they do like to go to museums. Our local museum doesn't charge admission on Tuesday evenings, so every Tuesday they eat an early dinner and leave the house by 6:30 PM. Those Tuesday evenings are their favorite nights! When they come home, they are filled with excitement about paintings that inspired them. Now, do I always enjoy being with my parents? I don't when they are talking to me about chores and homework that I need to do. But, aside from those times, they're pretty cool parents. P.S. I was happy to share them with you!

ACTIVITY 15 Subject and X-Word Match-Ups #5

In "On the Evening of September 11th, 2001" (activity 12) some X-words are used to talk about 1 and some X-words are used to talk about 2 or many. Go back and write a 1 over the X-words that talk about 1 subject and a 2 over the X-words that talk about two or more subjects. (See Appendix B for a complete list of X-words that show 1 or 2 or many to help you.) Here is an example.

X-N1 **X-N2**

September 11, 2001 is a day never to be forgotten. People are still shaking their heads in disbelief. There are many thoughts that they share. We are hearing that many teachers were very brave. They were frightened but knew their students were depending on them. They are to be applauded because not one student was injured. All were escorted to safety.

There is one man who has done a terrific job of making people feel safe. He is Mayor Giuliani. He and his workers were trapped in a building and escaped through a side door. He was pictured running away from the falling debris. Many New Yorkers have said they have never seen the Mayor function so beautifully. He was in charge right from the first few moments. He and his staff are to be congratulated because they have made us all proud.

Of course the firemen and police officers are heroes as well. Many have lost their lives trying to rescue others. Those at Ground Zero do not want to stop looking for possible survivors. They don't believe anyone is alive, but they are determined to keep looking. The Police Commissioner has said that he was thrilled that there was very little looting, but looting was not on most people's minds.

What happens now? We need to be patient. President Bush has been placed in a very difficult situation. The World Trade Center tragedy is the worst attack directly on America that we have ever experienced. He and the members of his cabinet do know that. We are going to need to wait and allow them time to work on a response.

ACTIVITY 16 A Brief Word about Most *WH-* (information) Questions

Go back to activity 3 and ask for more information about the 20 yes/no questions that you answered "yes" to. Pick *WH-* questions (WHEN, WHERE, WHY, and HOW) that make sense. Be sure to make up brief answers to your questions that make sense, too. (Your answers do not have to be full sentences.) What do you notice about the X-words?

1. Why is it small? Because that's the way it was made.
2. ______
3. ______
4. ______
5. ______
6. ______
7. ______
8. ______
9. ______
10. ______
11. ______
12. ______
13. ______

ACTIVITY 17 **Practice Editing I**

Edit the following sentences, using the correction symbols to the right of each sentence to help you find the errors.

Adapted from **"The Necklace"**
by Guy de Maupassant

"What ^**is** the matter with you?" asked her husband.	**X?**
"I . . . I . . . I ~~did~~ **do** not see the necklace."	**Time**
They searched everywhere. They was unable to find it.	**SX**
"But if you have dropped it in the street, it should still be there."	**Time**
"Yes. Do you take the number of the cab?"	**Time**
"No. ^ you take the number of the cab?"	**X?**
"No. I ^ go over all the ground and see if I could find it."	**X? Time**
Her husband returned about seven. He has found nothing.	**Time**
"Tell your friend that the necklace were broken."	**SX**
"That ^ give us time to look for it."	**X?**
They don't find the necklace.	**Time**
They bought a new necklace. It is worth $40,000 francs.	**Time**
They was allowed to pay $36,000 francs.	**SX**

ACTIVITY 18 Practice Editing II

Edit the following sentences, using the correction symbols to the right of each sentence to help you find the errors.

Adapted from ***Charlotte's Web***
by E. B. White, pp. 1–3

Sentence	Symbol
"Where ~~are~~ **is** Papa going with that ax?"	**SX**
"Out to the lighthouse," replied Mrs. Arabel. "Some pigs are born last night."	**Time**
"I didn't see why he needs an ax," continued Fern.	**Time**
"Well," said Mother, "one of the pigs was a runt."	**Time**
"It ^ very small and weak."	**X?**
"So your father have decided to kill it."	**SX**
"Just because it are smaller than the others?" shrieked Fern.	**SX**
"Don't yell, Fern!" she said. "Your father was right."	**Time**
Fern pushed a chair out of the way and ran outdoors. The grass ^ wet.	**X?**
Fern's sneakers are sopping by the time she caught up with her father.	**Time**
"Please didn't kill it!" she sobbed.	**Time**
"It was unfair."	**Time**
"Fern," he said gently. "You ^ learn to control yourself."	**X?**
"Control myself?" yelled Fern. "This was a matter of life and death!"	**Time**
"The pig can't help being born small."	**Time**

ACTIVITY 19 **Practice Editing III**

Edit the following sentences, using the correction symbols to the right of each sentence to help you find the errors.

Adapted from ***Charlotte's Web***
by E. B. White, pp. 3–7

Sentence	Symbol
"All right," he said. "You go back to the house, and I ~~would~~ **will** bring the runt."	**Time**
When Mr. Arable returned to the house, Fern is upstairs changing her sneakers.	**Time**
He were carrying a carton under his arm.	**SX**
The carton wobbled, and there were a scratching noise.	**SX**
There, inside, looking up, is the newborn pig.	**Time**
Fern doesn't take her eyes off the tiny pig.	**Time**
"Oh, look at him! Don't he look perfect?	**SX**
At this moment, Fern's brother, Avery, has come in the room.	**Time**
"What was that?" he demanded.	**Time**
"What ^ Fern holding?"	**X?**
"Do you wash your face and hands Avery?" asked Mrs. Arable.	**Time**
"That pig ^ no bigger than a white rat!"	**X?**
"Hurry and eat. The school bus would be here soon."	**Time**
"I does want a pig, too," said Avery.	**SX**
"No, Fern is up at daylight, and I only give pigs to early risers."	**Time**
But Fern can't eat until her pig has had a drink.	**Time** **Time**
A minute later, Fern were sitting on the floor giving her pig a bottle.	**SX**
She is teaching it how to suck, and her brother and mother was watching.	**Time** **SX**

Section 2

• X-Words and Main Verbs
• Hidden X-Words
• Editing Practice

Key teaching points:

X-Words match 100% without exception with their main verb.

If you do not see an X-word, DOES, DO, or DID is hiding in the main verb.

ACTIVITY 20 X-Word and Main Verb Match-Ups #1

Put an X over the X-words in the sentences below. If an X-word has a main verb next to it, put a V over the main verb partner. There are 10 X-word and main verb match-ups.

"The King and the Bees"

X V **X V**

One day, King Solomon was sitting on his throne, and his great men were standing around him. Suddenly, the Queen of Sheba entered the room.

"My dear King," she said, "in my country, far, far away, I have heard there was no puzzle you could not solve." Then she held up in each hand a beautiful wreath of flowers that were so alike that no one could see any differences.

"Someone made one of these wreaths from flowers from your garden. Someone made the other wreath from artificial flowers, shaped and colored by a skillful artist. Now tell me, dear King, which is the true and which is the false wreath? I have heard that you are the wisest man in the world," she said, "so surely this simple thing should not puzzle you."

Then the King remembered something. He remembered that close by his window there was a vine filled with beautiful sweet flowers. He remembered that he had seen many bees flying among these flowers and gathering honey from them.

So, he said, "Open the window!"

The next moment, two bees flew eagerly in, and then . . . another and another. All flew to the flowers in the Queen's right hand. Not one of the bees so much as looked at those in her left hand.

"Dear Queen of Sheba, the bees have given you my answer," said Solomon.

And the Queen said, "You are wise, King Solomon. You gather knowledge from the little things which common men do not notice."

Now . . . Match up all the X-word and main verbs here:

X-WORD	MAIN VERB	X-WORD	MAIN VERB	X-WORD	MAIN VERB
was	sitting				
were	standing				

ACTIVITY 21 X-Word and Main Verb Match-Ups #2

Put an X over the X-words in the sentences below. If an X-word has a main verb next to it, put a V over the main verb partner. There are 27 X-word and main verb match-ups.

"Saving the Birds"

X V **X**
One day in spring, four men were riding on horseback along a country road. These men were lawyers,
X V **X V**
and they were going to the next town to attend court. It had rained, and the ground was very soft. Water was dripping from the trees, and the grass was wet.

As they were passing through a grove of small trees, they saw something in the wet grass.

"What's the matter?" asked the first lawyer, whose name was Speed.

"Oh, it's only some old robins!" said the second lawyer, whose name was Hardin. "The storm has blown two of the little ones out of the nest. They're too young to fly, and the mother bird is making a great fuss about it."

"What a pity! They'll die down there in the grass," said the third lawyer, whose name I can't remember.

"Oh, well! They're nothing but birds," said Mr. Hardin. "Why should we care?"

"Yes, why should we care?" said Mr. Speed.

The three men, as they passed, looked down and saw the little birds fluttering in the cold, wet grass. They saw the mother robin flying about, and crying to her mate. Then they rode on, talking and laughing as before. In a few minutes, they'd forgotten about the birds.

But the fourth lawyer, whose name was Abraham Lincoln, stopped. He got down from his horse and very gently took the little ones up in his big warm hands. They did not seem afraid, but chirped softly, as if they had known they were safe.

➡ **more on next page**

ACTIVITY 21 *(continued from page 23)*

"Never mind, my little fellows," said Mr. Lincoln, "I will put you in your own cozy little bed." Then he looked up to find the nest from which they had fallen. It was high, much higher than he could reach. But Mr. Lincoln could climb. He had climbed many trees when he was a boy. He put the birds softly into their warm little home.

Soon the three lawyers who had ridden ahead stopped at a spring to give their horses water.

"Where is Lincoln?" asked one.

"Do you remember those birds?" asked Mr. Speed. "Very likely he has stopped to take care of them."

In a few minutes, Mr. Lincoln joined them. He had torn his coat on the thorny tree and had gotten mud all over his shoes.

"Hello, Abraham!" said Mr. Hardin. "Where have you been?"

"Gentlemen," said Mr. Lincoln, "I would not sleep tonight if I had left those helpless little robins to perish in the wet grass."

Now . . . Match up all the X-word and main verbs here:

X-WORD	MAIN VERB	X-WORD	MAIN VERB	X-WORD	MAIN VERB
were	**riding**				
were	**going**				
had	**rained**				

ACTIVITY 22 X-Word and Main Verb Match-Ups #3

Group the main verbs from "The King and the Bees" (activity 20) and "Saving the Birds" (activity 21) into the following categories. **Don't repeat verbs.**

The Base Form (no endings on the verb)	**The *ing* Form (_*ing* ending on the verb)**	**The *D-T-N* Form (verb ends with *d*, *t* or *n*)**
1. solve	1. sitting	1. heard
2. see	2. standing	2. seen
3. puzzle	3.	3.
4.	4.	4.
5.	5.	5.
6.	6.	6.
7.	7.	7.
8.		8.
9.		9.
10.		10.
11.		11.
12.		12.
		13.
		14.
		15.

These main verb forms match 100% without exception to the X-word families:

do, does, did,
will, would, shall, should,
can, could,
may, might, must → **The Base Form** (solve, see, puzzle. . .)

am, is, are, was, were → **The *ing* Form** (sitting, standing . . .)

have, has, had → **The *D-T-N* Form** (heard, seen. . .)

Now . . . Check your X-word and main verb match-ups in activities 20 and 21 to see if they follow the 100% without exception promise!

ACTIVITY 23 X-Word and Main Verb Match-Ups #4

Put an X over the X-words in the sentences below. Then use Appendix C (first three columns) to fill in each blank with the correct main verb form. Complete the chart below by putting all of the main verbs into their form groups.

From **"Angels and Other Strangers"** in ***A Christmas Treasury***
by Katherine Paterson, pp. 57–58

Minutes after the letter came from Arlene, Jacob set out walking for Washington. He wondered how long it would (X) __take__ (TAKE) him to get there. Before the truck died, he could ________ (MAKE) it in an hour, but he'd never ________ (TRY) to walk it. At sixty he knew that he didn't ________ (HAVE) the endurance that he had once ________ (HAVE), but he was still a strong man. Perhaps he could ________ (GET) there by morning if he kept a steady pace. Or if he could at least ________ (REACH) a place where there was a bus, he could ________ (RIDE) as far as the few bills in his pocket could ________ (TAKE) him.

Arlene needed him, so he would ________ (GO) to her if he needed to walk every step of the way. Arlene, his baby granddaughter, whom it seemed he had recently ________ (STOP) bouncing on his knee, was ________ (GO) to have a baby herself. She was alone and scared in the city and wanted her granddaddy, so he had ________ (PUT [ON]) his dead wife's overcoat and then his own and started out. The two coats protected him from the wet snow, but his wife's was too small and cut under his arms.

"I'm ________ (COME), Arlene baby," he said to the country road. "I'm ________ (GO) to be with you for Christmas."

BASE FORMS ______ ______ ______ ______ ______ ______ ______ ______

***ING* FORMS** __________ __________ __________

***D, T, N* FORMS** ________ ________ ________ ________

➡ How many main verb base forms did you find? 8, I hope!

How many main verb *ing* forms did you find? 3, I hope!

How many main verb *d*, *t*, or *n* forms did you find? 4, I hope!

ACTIVITY 24 X-Word and Main Verb Match-Ups #5

Put an X over the X-words in the sentences below. Then use Appendix C (first three columns) to fill in each blank with the correct main verb form. Complete the chart below by putting all of the main verbs into their form groups.

"The Glass Dog"

An accomplished wizard once lived on the top floor of a tenement house and passed his time in thoughtful study. He possessed all the books and recipes of all the wizards who had lived (LIVE) before him and even had ________ (INVENT) several magic potions himself.

People were always ____________ (INTERRUPT) his studies to consult him about their troubles. There would also _____ (BE) loud knocks from delivery men that were very __________ (DISTRACT). These interruptions aroused his anger, and he decided he must ______ (HAVE) a dog to keep people away from his door. He didn't ______ (KNOW) where to find a dog, but in the next room lived a poor glass-blower who he had _______ (KNOW) for several years. So, he went into the man's apartment and asked, "Where can I ______ (FIND) a dog?"

"What sort of a dog?" inquired the glass-blower.

"A good dog. One that will ______ (BARK) at people and will ______ (DRIVE) them away. One that will _____ (BE) no trouble to keep and won't _______ (EXPECT) to be fed. One that doesn't ______ (HAVE) fleas and is neat in his habits. One that will ______ (OBEY) me when I speak to him.

"Such a dog is hard to find," said the glass-blower who was _______ (MAKE) a blue flower pot with a pink glass rosebush in it.

Why can't you _______ (MAKE) me a dog out of glass?" he asked.

"I can," declared the glass-blower, "but it would not ______ (BARK) at people, you know."

"Oh, I'll _____ (FIX) that easily enough," replied the other. "If I could not _______ (MAKE) a glass dog bark, I would _____ (BE) a very poor wizard.

➡ more on next page

ACTIVITY 24 *(continued from page 27)*

BASE FORMS _______ _______ _______ _______ _______ _______ _______ _______

_______ _______ _______ _______ _______ _______________ _______

***ING* FORMS** _______________ _______________________________ _______________

***D-T-N* FORMS** _______________________ _______________ _______________________

➡ How many main verb base forms did you find? 15, I hope!

How many main verb *ing* forms did you find? 3, I hope!

How many main verb *d*, *t*, or *n* forms did you find? 3, I hope!

ACTIVITY 25 X-Word and Main Verb Match-Ups #6

Put an X over the X-words in the sentences below. Then use Appendix C (first three columns) to fill in each blank with the correct main verb form. Complete the chart below by putting all the main verbs into their form groups.

From: ***Red Scarf Girl: A Memoir of the Cultural Revolution***
by Ji Li Jiang, pp. 11–12

Principal Long was ___________ (READ) a newspaper. She raised her head and peered through her glasses to see who had ______________ (INTERRUPT) her. "Principal Long, here is a note from my father." I hurried out of the office before she could ________ (LOOK) at it or ask me any questions. I ran down the hallway, colliding with someone and running blindly on, thinking only that she must ______ (BE) very disappointed.

My best friend, An Yi, and our homeroom teacher were ____________ (STAND) outside the main building. As soon as they saw me, An Yi shouted, "Where have you ________ (BE)? Hurry up! You're _________ (GO) to be late."

I opened my mouth but couldn't _______ (SAY) a word.

"I . . . I'm not _________ (GO)." I bowed my head and twisted my fingers in my red scarf.

I did not _________ (RAISE) my head. I didn't _________ (WANT) to see An Yi's face.

I tried hard not to cry. Father wouldn't _______ (LET) me.

BASE FORMS ____________ _________ _________ _________ _________ _________

***ING* FORMS** ____________ _________ _________ _________

***D-T-N* FORMS** ____________ _________

➡ How many main verb base forms did you find? 6, I hope!

How many main verb *ing* forms did you find? 4, I hope!

How many main verb *d*, *t*, or *n* forms did you find? 2, I hope!

ACTIVITY 26 Hidden X-Words in Main Verbs: The Powerful X-Word *Does* #1

V/XS
Bob loves Mary.
Where is the X-word? The *s* on the main verb *love* means that the X-word *does* is hiding inside it, ready to do lots of work.

Here is the proof:

Yes/No Question: Does Bob love Mary?

Negative Statement: Bob doesn't love Mary.

Emphatic Statement: Bob does love Mary!

Find the hidden DOES X-word in the sentences below and place a V/XS over it. Then change it to make a YES/NO QUESTION, a NEGATIVE STATEMENT, and an EMPHATIC STATEMENT with an X over the X-word and a V over the main verb. Here is an example:

V/XS
The teacher lives in Virginia.

Yes/No Question: Does (X) the teacher live (V) in Virginia?

Negative Statement: The teacher doesn't (X) live (V) in Virginia.

Emphatic Statement: The teacher does (X) live (V) in Virginia!

She works at the Maryland School for the Deaf.

Yes/No Question: ______________________________

Negative Statement: ______________________________

Emphatic Statement: ______________________________

ACTIVITY 27 Hidden X-Words in Main Verbs: The Powerful X-Word *Does* #2

Here is more practice with the hidden X-word DOES. Find the hidden DOES X-words in the sentences below and place a V/XS over them. Then change each to make a YES/NO QUESTION, a NEGATIVE STATEMENT, and an EMPHATIC STATEMENT with an X over the X-word and a V over the main verb. The first two sets are done for you. **All sentences talk about NOW time and about 1 subject. The main verbs look like X-words, but they mean *to own something* (*have*) or *to physically do some action* (*do*). They are not X-words.**

V/XS (yes, *has* is the main verb here. It means "to own something.")
The boy has a lot of homework.

	X V
Yes/No Question:	Does the boy have a lot of homework?
	X V
Negative Statement:	The boy doesn't have a lot of homework.
	X V
Emphatic Statement:	The boy does have a lot of homework!

V/XS (yes, *does* is the main verb here. It means "to do something.")
He does his homework in the morning.

	X V
Yes/No Question:	Does he do his homework in the morning?
	X V
Negative Statement:	No, he doesn't do his homework in the morning.
	X V
Emphatic Statement:	He does do his homework in the morning!

The dog has an appointment with a vet for an x-ray.

Yes/No Question: ______________________________

Negative Statement: ______________________________

Emphatic Statement: ______________________________

The vet does the x-ray in his office.

Yes/No Question: ______________________________

Negative Statement: ______________________________

Emphatic Statement: ______________________________

ACTIVITY 28 Hidden X-Words in Main Verbs: The Powerful X-Word *Do* #1

V/XO
Bob and Fred love Mary.

Where is the X-word? No ending on the main verb LOVE means that the X-word DO is hiding inside it. Nothing (O) shows.

Here is the proof:

Yes/No Question: Do Bob and Fred love Mary?

Negative Statement: Bob and Fred don't love Mary.

Emphatic Statement: Bob and Fred do love Mary!

Find the hidden DO X-words in the two sentences below and place a V/XO over them. Then change each to make a YES/NO QUESTION, a NEGATIVE STATEMENT, and an EMPHATIC STATEMENT, with an X over the X-word and a V over the main verb. The first set is done for you.

V/XO
The teachers live in Virginia.

Yes/No Question: Do (**X**) the teachers live (**V**) in Virginia?

Negative Statement: The teachers don't (**X**) live (**V**) in Virginia.

Emphatic Statement: The teachers do (**X**) live (**V**) in Virginia!

They work at the Maryland School for the Deaf.

Yes/No Question: ______________________________

Negative Statement: ______________________________

Emphatic Statement: ______________________________

ACTIVITY 29 Hidden X-Words in Main Verbs: The Powerful X-Word *Do* #2

Here is more practice with the hidden X-word DO. Find the hidden DO X-words in the sentences below and place a V/XO over them. Then change each to make a YES/NO QUESTION, a NEGATIVE STATEMENT, and an EMPHATIC STATEMENT, with an X over the X-word and a V over the main verb. The first two sets are done for you. **All sentences talk about NOW time and about 2 or many subjects. The main verbs look like X-words, but they mean *to own something* (*have*) or *to physically do some action* (*do*). They are not X-words.**

V/XO (*have* is the main verb here. It means "to own something.")
The boys have a lot of homework.

Yes/No Question: **X** Do the boys **V** have a lot of homework?

Negative Statement: The boys **X** don't **V** have a lot of homework.

Emphatic Statement: The boys **X** do **V** have a lot of homework!

V/XO (*do* is the main verb here. It means "to do something.")
The boys do their homework in the morning.

Yes/No Question: **X** Do the boys **V** do their homework in the morning?

Negative Statement: The boys **X** don't **V** do their homework in the morning.

Emphatic Statement: The boys **X** do **V** do their homework in the morning!

Some children have problems getting along with their parents.

Yes/No Question: ______________________________

Negative Statement: ______________________________

Emphatic Statement: ______________________________

Parents do their best to raise good kids.

Yes/No Question: ______________________________

Negative Statement: ______________________________

Emphatic Statement: ______________________________

ACTIVITY 30 Finding Hidden *Does* and *Do*

Mark every X-word, but this time look for 9 hidden *does* and 6 hidden *do* X-words. Mark V/XS over the hidden *does* X-words and V/XO over the hidden *do* X-words. If you see the word *to* next to a base-form verb, circle the *to* and the base-form verb and label the circle INF, as shown below with *to save*, to mean *infinitive*. Remember to box all your subjects and to label all X-V matches. List all V/XS and V/XO in groups. **The passage talks about NOW time and about things that happen in general every day.**

Bob and Mary

X **V/XS**

It is no secret. Bob really loves Mary. He emails her every night and they write back and forth. They are in most of the same classes, so they get some of the same homework. But Bob takes science and Mary takes business math. They enjoy lunch time when they can see each other. Mary insists on eating in the cafeteria because she is trying **Inf** to save money. Bob prefers to eat at McDonald's because he says the food is better. 1. They do both. Sometimes they stay in school and sometimes they go out.

2. Bob has a part-time job. He can afford to treat Mary. But Mary is very considerate. She only allows Bob to pay once in a while.

V/XS loves ____ ____ ____ ____ ____ ____ ____ ____

V/XO ____ ____ ____ ____ ____ ____

Tricky, tricky, tricky!

Change sentences 1 and 2 into yes/no questions. Where are the X-words and main verbs? Mark them.

1. ____________________

2. ____________________

ACTIVITY 31 Hidden X-Words in Main Verbs: The Powerful X-Word *Did* #1

V/XD
Bob loved Mary. Where is the X-word?
The *d* on the main verb *love* means that the X-word *did* is hiding inside it.

Here is the proof:

Yes/No Question: Did Bob love Mary?

Negative Statement: Bob didn't love Mary.

Emphatic Statement: Bob did love Mary!

Find the hidden DID X-Words in the two sentences below and place a V/XD over them. Then change each to make a YES/NO QUESTION, a NEGATIVE STATEMENT, and an EMPHATIC STATEMENT, with an X over the X-word and a V over the main verb. The first set is done for you.

V/XD
The teacher lived in Virginia.

Yes/No Question: Did (X) the teacher live (V) in Virginia?

Negative Statement: No, the teacher didn't (X) live (V) in Virginia.

Emphatic Statement: The teacher did (X) live (V) in Virginia!

She and a neighbor worked at MSD.

Yes/No Question: ______________________________

Negative Statement: ______________________________

Emphatic Statement: ______________________________

Both of them drove to school together each morning.

Yes/No Question: ______________________________

Negative Statement: ______________________________

Emphatic Statement: ______________________________

ACTIVITY 32 Hidden X-Words in Main Verbs: The Powerful X-Word *Did* #2

Here is more practice with the hidden X-word DID. Find the hidden DID X-words in the sentences below and place a V/XD over them. Then change each to make a YES/NO QUESTION, a NEGATIVE STATEMENT, and an EMPHATIC STATEMENT, with an X over the X-word and a V over the main verb. **The main verbs look like X-words, but they mean *to own something (have)* or *to physically do some action* (*do*). They are not X-words.**

V/XD (*had* is the main verb here. It means "to own something.")
The boy had a lot of homework.

Yes/No Question: **X** Did the boy **V** have a lot of homework?

Negative Statement: The boy **X** didn't **V** have a lot of homework.

Emphatic Statement: The boy **X** did **V** have a lot of homework!

V/XD (*Did* is the main verb here. It means "to do something.")
He did his homework in the morning.

Yes/No Question: **X** Did he **V** do his homework in the morning?

Negative Statement: No, he **X** didn't **V** do his homework in the morning.

Emphatic Statement: Yes, he **X** did **V** do his homework in the morning!

The boy and girl had fun cleaning the house.

Yes/No Question: ______________________________

Negative Statement: ______________________________

Emphatic Statement: ______________________________

The girl had a lot of washing and ironing.

Yes/No Question: ______________________________

Negative Statement: ______________________________

Emphatic Statement: ______________________________

The boy did the cooking.

Yes/No Question: ______________________________

Negative Statement: ______________________________

Emphatic Statement: ______________________________

ACTIVITY 33 Finding Hidden *Did*

Mark every X-word as you have done before, but this time look for 10 hidden *did* X-words. Mark V/XD over the hidden *did* X-words. If you see the word *to* next to a *base-form verb*, circle the *to* and the *base-form verb* and label the circle INF, to mean *infinitive*, as shown below with *to smile*. Remember to box all your subjects and label all X-V matches. **List all V/XD in a group. The passage talks about BEFORE time and about completed actions, events, or feelings.**

Bob and Mary

V/XD over "Bob met"; **X** over "they were"; **Inf** over "to smile"

Bob met Mary when they were in junior high school. They were both on the swim team. At first they just looked at each other, but soon they started to smile at each other. It took Bob a few weeks to have the courage to ask Mary out. They lived near each other, so it wasn't hard for them to take the bus to the mall and to hang out there for several hours on the weekends. But soon Bob needed money for college and Mary was getting a lot of homework, so they saw less and less of each other on the weekends during high school. But, they saw each other in the hallways and at lunch. **1.** They also had one class together. **2.** They did their homework together too.

V/XD **met** ________ ________ ________ ________

________ ________ ________ ________ ________

➧ Tricky, tricky, tricky!

Change sentences 1 and 2 into yes/no questions. Where are the X-words and main verbs? Mark them.

1. ________________________

2. ________________________

ACTIVITY 34 **Finding X-Words, X-Word and Main Verb Match-Ups, and Hidden X-Words #1**

Put an X over all the alone X-words, XV over all the X-word main-verb match-ups, and either V/XS, V/XO, or V/XD over all the hidden X-words. The first two sentences are done for you. There are 5 alone X-words, 18 X-word main-verb match-ups, 3 V/XS, 4 V/XO, and 9 V/XD hidden X-words, counting repeats and the ones done for you. Circle and label all infinitives INF. List all the X-words and main verbs in groups.

"The Midnight Ride"

V/XD (over "happened")
The midnight ride of Paul Revere happened April 18/April 19, 1775—a long time ago when the king

V/XD (over "ruled") **X** (over "were")
of England ruled this country. There were thousands of English soldiers in Boston. The king had sent them there to force the people to obey his unjust laws. The soldiers guarded the streets of the town and didn't allow anyone to come in or to go out without their permission. People would say, "The king makes us pay taxes but he gives us nothing in return. He sends soldiers among us to take away our liberty. We do not wish to fight against the king, but we are free men, and he must not send soldiers to oppress us. We need to be ready to defend ourselves if the soldiers try to harm us."

A group of men were not afraid of the king's soldiers. They camped in Charlestown, a village near Boston, and from its hills, they could watch what the king's soldiers were doing. The men decided to buy gun powder and to store it in Concord, a city about 20 miles away, to protect themselves.

Paul Revere was one of the men who was watching the English soldiers. One day, a friend of his who was living in Boston secretly left and came to see him in Charlestown. He said, "I have something to tell you. Some of the king's soldiers are going to Concord to get the gun powder. They are getting ready to start tonight."

"Indeed!" said Paul Revere. "They'll get no gun powder if I can help it. I'll summon all the farmers between Charlestown and Concord to get their guns and axes to stand up to the redcoats. You'll hang a lantern in the tower of the Old North Church in Boston if the soldiers are starting out by land. If they cross the Charles River, you'll hang two lanterns."

➧ **more on next page**

ACTIVITY 34 *(continued from page 38)*

And with the second light from the second lantern, Paul Revere knew which way the soldiers were heading. He was ready to alert the farmers.

Alone X-Words _____ _____ _____ _____ _____

X-V Matches _____ _____ _____ _____ _____

_____ _____ _____ _____ _____

_____ _____ _____ _____ _____

__________ _____ __________

V/XS __________ __________ _____

V/XO _____ _____ _____ __________

V/XD _____ _____ _____ _____ _____

_____ _____ _____ __________

ACTIVITY 35 Finding X-Words, X-Word and Main Verb Match-Ups, and Hidden X-Words #2

Put an X over all the alone X-words, XV over all the X-word main-verb match-ups, and either V/XS, V/XO, or V/XD over all the hidden X-words. The first two sentences are done for you. There are 8 alone X-words, 15 X-word main-verb match-ups, 2 V/XS, 6 V/XO, and 27 V/XD hidden X-words, counting repeats and the ones done for you. Circle and label all infinitives INF. List all the X-words and main verbs in groups.

"The Story of a Great Story"

V/XD **X**

Alexander Selkirk lived in Scotland almost 300 years ago. He was quarrelsome and unruly, often making trouble among his neighbors. When he ran away and went to sea, many people were glad and said, "We hope he gets what he deserves." He became a fine sailor, but he was often in trouble with the other sailors, and even the captain, for being disagreeable.

Once his ship was sailing in the great Pacific Ocean. It was four hundred miles from the coast of South America when something happened which Selkirk did not like. He screamed, "I need to get off this ship. I would rather live alone on a desert island."

"Very well," answered the captain. "We will drop you off on the first island that we see."

The very next day, they saw a little green island with groves of trees near the shore and high hills beyond them.

"I want you to leave me there. I only need a few common tools and some food, and I will do well enough for several weeks."

"You may have your wish," answered the captain.

Alexander Selkirk was all alone on the island, and he began to see how foolish he had been; he thought how terrible it would be to live there without one friend, without one person to whom he could speak. Sometimes Selkirk noticed ships sailing in the distance, and he tried to signal them; he called them as loudly as he could, but no one heard, and the ships did not come. For four years and four months he lived alone on the island. "If I ever have the good fortune to escape from this island,"

➡ **more on next page**

he said, "I will be kind and considerate to everyone. I will try to make friends instead of enemies." Then to his great joy, a ship came nearer and anchored in the little harbor. He explained who he was, and the captain willingly agreed to take him back to his own country. When he reached Scotland, everybody was eager to hear about his adventures, and he soon found himself famous. A writer in England heard how Selkirk had lived alone on an island and decided it would make a wonderful story. He called his story, "The Adventures of Robinson Crusoe" and almost every child has read this famous story.

Alone X-Words ________ ________ ________ ________ ________

________________ ________________ ________

X-V Matches ________ ________ ________ ________ ________

________ ________ ________ ________ ________

________ ________ ________ ________ ________

V/XS ________________ ________________________

V/XO ________ ________ ________ ________ ________

____

V/XD ________ ________ ________ ________ ________

________ ________ ________ ________ ________

________ ________ ________ ________ ________

________ ________ ________ ________ ________

________ ________ ________ ________ ________

________________ ________________

ACTIVITY 36 Practice Editing I

Edit the following sentences using the correction symbols on the right of each sentence to help you find the errors.

1. Shira is looked for her dog. **XV**

____

2. All week Cubby was so upset in school. He fights with his friends. **V/XD**

____

____

3. Also I'm begun to thinking about her. **XV INF**

____

4. Many people love it there. Plus, they has skiing too. **V/XO**

____

5. He had a lot of hard work in Vietnam. He has a lot of jobs, and he survives it all. **V/XD V/XD**

____

____

6. He just like to takes some risks. **V/XS INF**

____

7. My heart was beaten rapidly. **XV**

____

8. Dr. Cuss did hitted a man's sleeve, but there no arm. But, did felt something. **XV X? S? XV**

____

____

ACTIVITY 37 Practice Editing II

Edit the following sentences using the correction symbols on the right of each sentence to help you find the errors.

Adapted from ***Charlotte's Web***
by E. B. White, pp. 5–7

1. Fern couldn't ate until her pig had some milk. **XV**

2. Mrs. Arable finds a baby's bottle and a rubber nipple. **V/XD**

3. Fern taught the pig to sucking from the bottle. **INF**

4. The pig have a good appetite. **V/XD**

5. The school bus was arriving. **V/XD**

6. Fern is thinking about a name for her pig. **Time**

7. She didn't noticed the children on the bus. **XV**

8. "I will named my pig Wilbur," said Fern. **XV**

9. "Do you had a pig?" asked a child on the bus. **XV**

10. "Yes, I did have a pig," said Fern. **Time**

➧ **more on next page**

ACTIVITY 37 *(continued from page 43)*

11. "Why did you picked Wilbur for a name?" asked the child. **XV**

____

12. "I liked the name Wilbur," said Fern. **V/XO**

____

13. "It make the pig more human." **V/XS**

____

14. "I takes care of it, and I feeds it everyday." **V/XO V/XO**

____

15. "Where the pig sleep?" asked the child. **X?**

____

16. "The pig sleep in the barn," says Fern. **V/XS V/XD**

____

ACTIVITY 38 **Practice Editing III**

Edit the following sentences using the correction symbols on the right of each sentence to help you find the errors.

From **"Let's Trade"** in ***Reading for Concepts, Book A***, p. 38

1.	Long ago, people had to getting what they want by trading.	**INF V/XD**
2.	Some people farm the land.	**V/XD**
3.	Other people make tools.	**V/XD**
4.	People trade tools for food.	**V/XD**
5.	If people had too much meat, they could traded it for corn.	**XV**
6.	Many people want beautiful things.	**V/XD**
7.	A farmer would trades milk for a piece of beautiful cloth.	**XV**
8.	Even today we traded with one another.	**V/XO**
9.	When you buy candy, did you pay for it with bear fat?	**Time**
10.	Of course not! You used money.	**V/XO**

➡ **more on next page**

11. But you are still trade. **XV**

____

12. You were still giving one thing for another. **Time**

____

ACTIVITY 39 **Practice Editing IV**

Edit the following sentences using the correction symbols on the right of each sentence to help you find the errors.

Adapted from **"What Is It Worth?"** in ***New Practice Readers: Book B***
by Donald G. Anderson, pp. 118–119

1. As you know, at one time, different countries use different measures. **V/XD**

____

2. But even inside the same country, measures was not always the same. **SX**

____

3. When America was very young, each colony has its own money. **V/XD**

____

4. The coins did not had the same worth. **XV**

____

5. Other money comes from countries such as Spain, France and Portugal. **V/XD**

____

6. People become confused. **V/XD**

____

7. They would bought things. **XV**

____

8. But they can not be sure if they have their money's worth. **Time V/XD**

____

9. Then, one of our first presidents, Thomas Jefferson, thinks of a good plan. **V/XD**

____

10. He was started the dollar system. ~~X~~

____

➡ **more on next page**

11. People learned count by tens. **INF**

____

12. Ten cents make a dime. Ten dimes make a dollar. **V/XD V/XD**

____

13. Today, we still used Jefferson's plan. **V/XO**

____

Section 3

• Sentence Patterns

• Editing Practice

Key teaching points:

Trunks are basic sentences to which other trunks or sentence parts can be added.

How they are added determines punctuation.

ACTIVITY 40 Review of Changing Statements into Yes/No Questions

Change each of the following statements into YES/NO questions. Label the statements and questions as shown. **Remember: If you see an X-word, move it in front of the subject. If you do not see an X-word, it is hidden. Pull the hidden X-word (either *does, do,* or *did*) out of its main verb and move it in front of the subject too.**

1. This **(X)** is a good class.

   (X) Is this a good class?

2. All the students learned **(V/XD)** a lot.

   (X) Did all the students learn **(V)** a lot?

3. One girl studies **(V/XD)** four hours each day.

   (X) Does one girl study **(V)** four hours each day?

4. She will pass this class.

   ____

5. Most students study only one hour.

   ____

6. There are two teachers.

   ____

7. Both teachers work very hard.

   ____

8. They want their students to learn.

   ____

9. My brothers had both teachers.

   ____

10. They liked them.

    ____

11. The teachers gave them a lot of help.

    ____

12. One teacher will retire.

    ____

13. She wants to live in Florida.

    ____

14. The other teacher will continue on.

    ____

15. She has lots of new ideas.

    ____

16. One idea is to use more technology.

    ____

ACTIVITY 41 What Is a Trunk?

A trunk is a basic English sentence—a sentence without any "extras"—like one that tells when or why. It is a subject and a predicate with only one main verb. It can easily turn into a yes/no question. Make trunks by matching the subjects (on the left) with the predicates (on the right) that make sense. Start each trunk with a capital letter and end with a period. Use the lines below to write your trunks.

TRUNK

SUBJECT	**PREDICATE**
The Maryland School for the Deaf	freezes at 32 degrees Fahrenheit
Washington, D.C.	are the Yankees and the Mets
Serious students	is impossible to read in the dark
There	can be fun
Water	is the capital of the United States
It	are a billion people living in China
Learning to cook	has two campuses
The two New York baseball teams	are in middle school
Sixth, seventh, and eighth graders	always come to class on time

TRUNK

1. The Maryland School for the Deaf has two campuses.
2. ____________________
3. ____________________
4. ____________________
5. ____________________
6. ____________________
7. ____________________
8. ____________________
9. ____________________

ACTIVITY 42 Changing Trunks into Yes/No Questions

In your mind, change trunks 1–9 in activity 41 into yes/no questions. Did it work? Now write 5 of your own trunks below and change each to a yes/no question.

1. ______________________________

____

2. ______________________________

____

3. ______________________________

____

4. ______________________________

____

5. ______________________________

____

➡ Did each trunk turn into a yes/no question?

ACTIVITY 43 **Joining Trunks: T, + T with *and***

Join the following trunks with the joiner word *and*. Make sure each trunk can turn into a yes/no question. You'll need a comma before the joiner word. Label each sentence T, + T as shown. Write Ts over the verbs or X-words in the sentences.

1. Peter and Sue wanted to buy a car.
   They wanted to buy one quickly.

   T , + T
   Peter and Sue wanted to buy a car, and they wanted to buy one quickly.

2. They read the ads in newspapers.
   They looked in showrooms.

3. Peter asked his friends at work.
   Sue posted a sign in their apartment building.

4. Peter received no responses at work.
   No one responded to Sue's sign.

5. They saw a car with a "For Sale" sign in its window.
   They asked the owner how much the car cost.

6. The car was pretty new.
   It was the right price. Sold!

➡ In a T, + T pattern, the joiner word *and* can be replaced with a semi-colon as seen below.

Peter and Sue wanted to buy a car, and they wanted to buy one quickly.

Peter and Sue wanted to buy a car; they wanted to buy one quickly.

ACTIVITY 44 Joining Trunks: T, + T with *but*

But shows contrasting ideas between two trunks. Join a trunk from the left with a trunk from the right that makes sense, using the joiner word *but*. Make sure each trunk can turn into a yes/no question. You'll need a comma before the joiner word. Write 7 good sentences in the blanks below. Label each sentence T, + T as shown.

T	**T**
I studied hard	people call me Susan
Computers are remarkable	she was able to find her keys quickly
The driver wasn't hurt	it felt more like summer
The room was a mess	the homework was still due
My real name is Sue	the car was destroyed
It was winter	I failed anyway
The teacher was absent	they can't think for people

T , + T

1. I studied hard, but I failed anyway.

2. ____________________

3. ____________________

4. ____________________

5. ____________________

6. ____________________

7. ____________________

ACTIVITY 45 **Joining Trunks: T, + T with *so***

So shows the result or effect of a first trunk. Join a first trunk from the left with a result or effect trunk from the right that makes sense, using the joiner word *so*. Make sure each trunk can turn into a yes/no question. You'll need a comma before the joiner word. Write 7 good sentences in the blanks below. Label each sentence T, + T as shown.

T	**T**
The teacher caught the students cheating	she stayed up all night reading it
The airplane tickets were too expensive	they decided to stay indoors
The books were overdue	they decided to drive
Peter and Sue love warm weather	she called their parents
Olivia was gaining too much weight	we returned them to the library
The snow fell at the rate of one inch per hour	she threw out the ice cream
The book was incredibly interesting	they bought a home in Florida

T **, +** **T**

1. The teacher caught the students cheating, so she called their parents.
2. ______________________________
3. ______________________________
4. ______________________________
5. ______________________________
6. ______________________________
7. ______________________________

ACTIVITY 46 Joining Trunks: T, + T with *or*

Or trunks talk about an additional choice from a first trunk. Join a first trunk from the left with a different choice or result trunk from the right that makes sense, using the joiner word *or*. Make sure each trunk can turn into a yes/no question. You'll need a comma before the joiner word. Write 7 good sentences in the blanks below. Label each sentence T, + T as shown.

T	T
We'll go to the theater	it will receive an F
They'll fly to Las Vegas	you'll get a headache later
The essay needs to be rewritten	they'll go by train
She'll work in the city as a dog walker	he'll wait until the spring
He'll play soccer in the fall	she'll work at the beach as a babysitter
He'll either go to the movies	he'll go to the bowling alley
You should eat something now	we'll go bowling

T , + T

1. We'll go to the theater, or we'll go bowling.
2. ______________________________
3. ______________________________
4. ______________________________
5. ______________________________
6. ______________________________
7. ______________________________

ACTIVITY 47 **Practice with Joiners**

Join each pair of trunks with a comma and the joiner that makes the most sense. Choose *AND*, *BUT*, *SO*, or *OR*. Label each T, + T.

1. I prepared the dinner.
   Peter cleaned up after it.

   T **, +** **T**
   I prepared the dinner, and Peter cleaned up after it.

2. We invited them to come.
   They had other things to do.

   ____

3. My husband was sick.
   We decided not to go to the party.

   ____

4. You'll need to cover the candy.
   The ants won't crawl all over it.

   ____

5. We were hungry.
   We bought some food.

   ____

6. The dog needs to go out.
   It will do something on the rug.

   ____

7. Living in a dorm is fun.
   It's a great way to make friends.

   ____

8. Students need to read 100 pages a week.
   Their vocabulary will not improve.

   ____

ACTIVITY 48 **One Trunk with Two Predicates: T =**

Here are some T, +T patterns from activities 43–46 where the subjects of each trunk are the same:

T, + T *They* read the ads in newspapers, and *they* looked in showrooms.

T, + T *The car* was pretty new, and *it* was the right price.

T, + T *I* studied hard, but *I* failed anyway.

T, + T *It* was winter, but *it* felt more like summer.

T, + T *The essay* needs to be rewritten, or *it* will receive an F.

If the subjects of two trunks are the same, you can drop the second subject and the comma. Then you have a T = pattern! T = patterns start with a verb or X-word after *and*, *but*, *so*, and *or*.

T = They read the ads in the newspapers and looked in showrooms.

T = The car was pretty new and was the right price.

T = I studied hard but failed anyway.

T = It was winter but felt more like summer.

T = The essay needs to be rewritten or will receive an F.

Change the following T, + T patterns into T = patterns:

T, + T The girl took the pencil, and she put it in a drawer.

T = The girl took the pencil and put it in a drawer.

T, + T Michael was a good friend, but he was sometimes dishonest.

T = ____________________

T, + T Jerry turned off the lights, but he couldn't fall asleep for a while.

T = ____________________

T, + T She wasn't feeling well, so she decided to leave.

T = ____________________

ACTIVITY 49 One Trunk with Three (or more) Predicates Joined by *and*

Trunks with three or more predicates joined by *and* need commas to separate all predicates:

The young mother fed the baby, washed the dishes, and went to bed.
He gets up every morning, brushes his teeth, washes his face, eats breakfast, and goes to work.
I come home, watch some television, eat a snack, and do my homework.

Combine the groups of sentences below into *one sentence each* using the pattern T =.

1. The two women borrowed money. They rented an office. They started their own business.

____

____

2. The two friends shopped for clothes.
They ate lunch out.
They took the subway home.

____

____

3. The students got the notes for the final exam.
They set up study groups.
They passed the course.

____

____

4. The teacher entered the room. She opened her bag. She passed out the test.

____

____

5. She had a headache.
She felt ill.
She fainted.

____

____

6. He was late for class.
He missed his presentation.
He realized he would fail the assignment.

____

____

ACTIVITY 50 Practice with T, + T and T =

Can you identify the sentence patterns below? Use T for a single trunk, T, + T for two trunks combined with a joiner word, and T= for one trunk with two or more predicates.

T It was the first snow of the season.

T = It started early in the morning and continued through the night.

T, + T It was supposed to stop at 3 a.m., but it continued on until the morning.

_______ Sarah woke up and wondered if her school would be closed.

_______ There hadn't been a snow day for a long, long time.

_______ The last one was seven years before.

_______ She was in kindergarten and remembered the day.

_______ She and her mom baked cookies in the morning, took a nap in the afternoon, and did some coloring in the evening.

_______ She was older now, so she wanted to spend the day with her friends.

_______ She wanted to videophone them but realized that the telephone lines were down.

_______ That meant no email as well.

_______ She turned on the television and read the captions about school closings.

_______ It was her lucky day!

_______ All schools in the county were closed!

_______ She got washed, got dressed, and thought about walking to her friend's house.

_______ She tried to open the front door, but it would not budge.

_______ The snow outside was up to the door knob!

_______ She closed the door and went upstairs to tell her mom.

_______ They decided to bake cookies.

_______ It was the perfect snow-day activity!

ACTIVITY 51 Sentence Combining with T, + T and T =

Combine the groups of sentences below into *one sentence each* using the patterns T, + T or T =. Watch out for capitals, periods, and commas.

"My Dog Twister"

1. I have a black Labrador retriever.
   Her name is Twister.

   ____

2. She was trained to assist blind people.
   She failed the final test.

   ____

   ____

3. She is not very friendly with other dogs.
   She loves people.

   ____

   ____

4. She has jet black fur.
   She has white around her paws.
   She has grey around her mouth.

   ____

5. She knows commands such as sit, stay, down, and come.
   She likes doing them.

   ____

   ____

6. She is never more than two inches away from me.
   I have to be careful not to step on her.

   ____

ACTIVITY 52 **Linkers and Trunks (LT)**

A linker connects the meaning of the sentence it begins with the meaning of the sentence before it. Let's see how some authors use linkers.

"The Hotel Owner's Mistake"

Some men were sitting by the door of a hotel in Baltimore. As they looked all the way down the street, they saw a farmer on horseback riding toward the hotel. He was riding very slowly, and both he and his horse were covered with mud. *Finally*, the farmer arrived at the hotel.

"Do you have a room here for me?" he asked the hotel owner.

Now the owner prided himself upon keeping a first-class hotel, and he feared that his guests would not like the rough-looking farmer. So, he answered, "No, sir. Every room is full. *However*, the only place I could put you would be in the barn."

"Well, *first*," answered the stranger, "I will see if there are empty rooms at the Planters' Tavern around the corner," and he rode away.

Later on, a well-dressed gentleman came into the hotel and said, "I wish to see Mr. Thomas Jefferson."

"Mr. Jefferson?" asked the owner, "the Vice President of the United States?"

"Yes," said the gentleman. "I met him as he rode into town, and he said that he intended to stop at this hotel."

"I turned Mr. Jefferson away because he was covered in mud. What an idiot I was! *Now*, I must run over to Planters' Tavern and bring him back."

So, he went to the other hotel, where he found the vice president sitting with some friends in the lobby. "Mr. Jefferson," he said, "I have come to ask your pardon. I thought you were some old farmer. Come back to my hotel, and I will give you the best room in the house."

"No," said Mr. Jefferson. "A farmer is as good as any other man. *Therefore*, if there is no room for a farmer, there can be no room for me."

ACTIVITY 53 Other Linkers and What They Mean

Note that linkers begin with a capital letter and are followed by a comma.

Linkers that mean AND:

L **T**

She likes to dance, sew, and skate. *In addition*, she enjoys working in the garden.

Linkers that mean BUT:

L **T**

He is allergic to chocolate. *However*, he continues to eat it.
Still,

Linkers that mean SO:

L **T**

They are missing three assignments. *As a result*, they may not go to the dance.
Therefore,

Linkers that mean DIFFERENT WAY:

L **T**

The project required a lot of time, money, and energy. *On the other hand*, it was an excellent learning experience.

Linkers that EXPLAIN:

L **T**

Fat-free foods are not free of calories. *In other words*, you can gain weight eating them.

Linkers that ADD ADDITIONAL DETAIL:

L **T**

She did very well in school this term. *In fact*, she got all As.
Actually,

ACTIVITY 54 Practice with Linkers

Which linker would make *the most* sense in the pairs of sentences below? Rewrite them with the linker. Use Appendix D to help you. Watch your periods, capitals, and commas. Label the linker *L* and the trunk *T*.

1. She struggled with the assignment. She got it!

   L **T**

   She struggled with the assignment. Finally, she got it!

2. He passed the test. He got the highest grade.

3. She likes to read, cook, and swim. She likes to watch old-time movies.

4. They like to camp out. They don't like to shower outdoors.

5. He never read the assigned books. He failed the class.

6. They decided not to go to the mall. They went to the gym.

7. They didn't enjoy staying in the house all day. They got a lot of chores done.

8. The spaghetti sauce was delicious. It was the best they had ever eaten.

9. She was told that she was late to work too many times and that the job would be given to someone else. She was fired.

ACTIVITY 55 Practice Editing for Sentence Patterns I

Errors in sentence patterns below are marked with correction symbols in the right margin. Correct the sentences just for the sentence patterns based on the correction symbols. The first two have been done for you.

1. We started to trust each other, expressed our secret personalities. **T=**

   We started to trust each other *and* expressed our secret personalities.

2. Interpreters did not show up. However, mainstream classes did not help me to improve. **T LT**

   Interpreters did not show up. *Therefore*, mainstream classes did not help me to improve.

3. An interpreter explained why she was absent, I still did not understand. **T, +T**

   ___

4. He had to know what he was supposed to do during the war. He went to boot camp to train for it. **T, +T**

   ___

   ___

5. He finished training in San Diego, California. He went and got on an air force plane to go to Vietnam. **T LT=**

   ___

   ___

6. We decided to ask him questions, we interviewed him. **T, +T**

   ___

7. Gino wagged his tail, and brought his toys to Tarlie, she smiled and played with him. **T= T=**

   ___

8. Gino and Tarlie spent the rest of their lives together and they were full of happiness, Tarlie thanked God for inventing animals. **T, +T T**

   ___

   ___

9. Teenagers want to act mature, but can act childish. **T, +T**

   ___

ACTIVITY 56 Practice Editing for Sentence Patterns II

Errors in sentence patterns are marked with correction symbols in the right margin. Correct the sentences just for the sentence patterns based on the correction symbols. The first two have been done for you.

1. It was their parents' 40th wedding anniversary so the son and daughter planned a surprise party. **T, +T**

   It was their parents' 40th wedding anniversary, so the son and daughter planned a surprise party.

2. The son and daughter were both in their twenties, and lived in the city. Their parents lived in a small town miles away. **T= LT**

   The son and daughter were both in their twenties and lived in the city. *However*, their parents lived in a small town miles away.

3. They wanted to have the party in their parents' town, they had to drive out to the small town several times to speak with restaurant owners. **T, +T**

   ______

   ______

4. The son preferred a luncheon. Therefore, the daughter wanted a dinner. **T LT**

   ______

5. They argued back and forth. In addition, they decided that a luncheon would save them money. **T LT**

   ______

6. The son and daughter wanted to write invitations by hand, there wasn't enough time. **T, +T**

   ______

7. They talked about calling the guests on the phone to invite them. In fact, they decided to use a Web site that allows guests to reply online to party invitations. **T LT**

   ______

   ______

➧ **more on next page**

ACTIVITY 56 *(continued from page 66)*

8. Only 50 people responded to the online invitation. Therefore, 75 people came to the party! **T LT**

____

9. The parents screamed with delight, and cried and felt overwhelmed on the day of the party. **T= = =**

____

10. They were not dressed appropriately, it was proof that they were surprised! **T, +T**

____

ACTIVITY 57 Front and End Shifters (FT and TE)

There are words or groups of words that can come before or after a trunk to add more information about the trunk. These words or groups of words can be shifted from the front of the trunk (FT) to the end of the trunk (TE) or from the end of the trunk (TE) to the front of the trunk (FT) without changing meaning. Shifters most often tell us WHEN, WHERE, or WHY about a trunk.

"Which Was the King?"

F **T**
On a beautiful day in May, King Henry the Fourth of France was hunting in a forest with a group of men.
T **E**
King Henry the Fourth of France was hunting in a forest with a group of men on a beautiful day in May.

F **T**
Because he wanted to enjoy the longer way back to town by himself, he told his men to ride home by the shorter main road.
T **E**
He told his men to ride home by the shorter main road because he wanted to enjoy the longer way back to town by himself.

F **T**
As he came out of the forest, he saw a little boy waiting patiently by the roadside.
T **E**
He saw a little boy waiting patiently by the roadside as he came out of the forest.

The little boy wanted to meet the king.

CAREFUL!! NOTHING TO SHIFT HERE.

T **E**
He was waiting patiently because he heard the king was hunting in the forest.
F **T**
Because he heard the king was hunting in the forest, he was waiting patiently.

F **T**
"If that is what you wish, you can ride with me to town," [said the king].
T **E**
"You can ride with me to town if that is what you wish," [said the king].

T (question) **E**
"How will I know who the king is if there are a lot of men surrounding him?" [asked the boy]
F **T (question)**
If there are a lot of men surrounding him, how will I know who the king is?" [asked the boy]

F **T**
"Except for the king, all the other men will take off their hats," [said the king].
T **E**
"All the other men will take off their hats except for the king," [said the king].

➡ **more on next page**

ACTIVITY 57 *(continued from page 68)*

F **T**
When the king and boy arrived at the main road, all the men seemed amused.
T **E**
All the men seemed amused when the king and boy arrived at the main road.

F **T**
As they usually do, the men greeted the king by taking off their hats.
T **E**
The men greeted the king by taking off their hats as they usually do.

T **E**
[The boy said,] "The king must be either you or I because we both have our hats on."
F **T**
[The boy said,] "Because we both have our hats on, the king must be either you or I."

➡ Which shifters need a comma: FT or TE? ____

Can shifters change into yes/no questions? YES or NO? ____

ACTIVITY 58 **Shifting Shifters**

Only shifters can shift. Shift the beginning of each sentence below to the end of the sentence and re-write it. If you can't shift anything, leave the space blank. Label your trunks and shifters.

Adapted from: ***Harvey Slumfenburger's Christmas Present***
by John Burningham

1. At last, Santa and the reindeer arrived home.

____

2. Because they had been delivering presents, the reindeer were tired.

____

3. All the children got presents.

____

4. After they ate, the reindeer went to bed.

____

5. One of the reindeer was not feeling well.

____

6. In the morning, it still was not feeling well.

____

7. Santa realized that one present for Harvey Slumfenburger was not delivered.

____

8. Without all the reindeer, how would Santa deliver the present?

____

9. While eating breakfast, Santa thought of a plan.

____

10. If he could get a little help from his neighbors, he would deliver the present without the reindeer.

____

➡ Which shifters need a comma: FT or TE? ____

Can shifters change into yes/no questions? YES or NO? _____

ACTIVITY 59 **Shifting Shifters**

Only shifters can shift. Shift the end of each sentence below to the front of the sentence and re-write it. Remember to add a comma after the front shifter. If you can't shift anything, leave the space blank. Label your trunks and shifters.

"Cinderella"

1. Cinderella stayed home and did all the housework while her stepsisters went to parties and balls.

____

____

2. Her name was Cinderella because she spent so much time cleaning the ashes and cinders.

____

3. Now it happened that the king was to give a ball.

____

4. The stepsisters were thrilled when they received an invitation.

____

5. They had sent for the best dressmaker by the end of the day.

____

6. Cinderella helped her stepsisters dress for the ball even though she was upset about not receiving an invitation.

____

____

7. Cinderella watched from the kitchen window as the stepsisters drove away in their fine carriage.

____

8. She sat down by the fire and began to cry when the carriage was out of sight.

____

➧ **more on next page**

9. She heard a voice from out of nowhere.

____

10. "You must listen carefully if you want to go to the ball."

____

11. "You'll need to bring me the largest pumpkin you can find from outside in the garden."

____

➡ Which shifters need a comma: FT or TE? ____

Can shifters change into yes/no questions? YES or NO? _____

ACTIVITY 60 **A Word about Fragments**

Turn each of the following into yes/no questions. If you can, write TRUNK. If you can't, write FRAGMENT.

1. It isn't easy to learn American Sign Language. **TRUNK**
   yes/no question: Isn't it easy to learn American Sign Language?
2. Because it's a different kind of language. **FRAGMENT**
   yes/no question: *Is because* it a different kind of language?
3. When people try to learn it. ______
   yes/no question: ______
4. They can express themselves well. ______
   yes/no question: ______
5. But have a hard time understanding it. ______
   yes/no question: ______
6. That's different from learning other languages. ______
   yes/no question: ______
7. Because understanding language is easier than expressing it. ______
   yes/no question: ______

➡ Fragments will never turn into yes/no questions because they are not trunks. They might be *shifters*!

Now change sentences 1 and 2 above into a TE pattern here:

______

Change sentences 3, 4, and 5 into a FT= pattern here:

______

Change sentences 6 and 7 into a TE pattern here:

______

______

ACTIVITY 61 **Another Word about Fragments**

Try to turn each of the following into yes/no questions. If you can, write TRUNK. If you can't, write FRAGMENT.

1. When I was a little girl. **FRAGMENT**
   yes/no question: *Was when* I a little girl?

2. I went to the beach everyday in the summer. **TRUNK**
   yes/no question: Did I go to the beach everyday in the summer?

3. If it was a sunny day. ______
   yes/no question: ______

4. At about noon time. ______
   yes/no question: ______

5. I ate meat, potatoes, and a vegetable. ______
   yes/no question: ______

6. Because my mother didn't want to cook a big meal. ______
   yes/no question: ______

7. When she came home from the beach. ______
   yes/no question: ______

8. We didn't realize that this was a healthy way to eat. ______
   yes/no question: ______

9. Because it was in the 1950s. ______
   yes/no question: ______

10. When many people didn't know about healthy lifestyles. ______
    yes/no question: ______

➡ Now change numbers 1 and 2 above into a FT pattern here:

______

Now change numbers 3, 4, 5, 6, and 7 into a FFTEE pattern here:

______

______

Now change numbers 8, 9, and 10 into a TEE pattern here:

______

______

______

ACTIVITY 62 **Inserts (TI)**

Inserts add interest to a sentence by adding detail in the middle or at the end of the sentence. You can remove an insert and the sentence will be complete and correct. Inserts do not shift. They always have punctuation on both sides.

From ***Homecoming***
by Cynthia Voigt, p. 14

T **I**
1. They had hamburgers and French fries and, *after Dicey thought it over*, milkshakes.

T **I**
2. They could have one more meal before they ran out of money, *or maybe two more.*

T **I**
3. The little ones horsed around in the back, *teasing, wrestling, tickling, quarreling, and laughing.*

Adapted from ***The Ant Bully***
by John Nickle, p. 1

T **I**
4. Sid, *the neighborhood bully*, was especially mean to Lucas.

T **I**
5. Lucas, *however*, was not mean to Sid.

T **I**
6. The Civil War *(1861–1865)* killed more Americans than any other war in history.

T **I**
7. There were several famous battles of the war: *Antietam, Bull Run, Gettysburg, and Vicksburg.*

T **I**
8. Abraham Lincoln, *president during the Civil War*, was respected throughout the world.

T **I**
9. Many people praised his kindly spirit—*even his enemies.*

➡ What punctuation can start or end inserts?

____

ACTIVITY 63 Inserting Inserts

Rewrite each sentence with the insert in the right place and with punctuation on both sides of the insert.

1. T: John Fitzgerald Kennedy was shot to death on November 22, 1963.
   I: the youngest man ever elected president

   ____

2. T: Kennedy won the presidency after several debates with his opponent.
   I: Vice President Richard M. Nixon.

   ____

3. T: Kennedy was the first president of the Roman Catholic faith.
   I: (1917–1963)

   ____

4. T: His parents moved the family to better neighborhoods.
   I: each time moving into bigger and better homes

   ____

5. T: They lived in a variety of cities.
   I: Brookline, Riverdale, and Bronxville

   ____

6. T: He entered Harvard in 1936.
   I: majoring in government and international relations

   ____

7. T: Jack spent 1939 traveling in Europe.
   I: as his family called him

   ____

8. T: *Why England Slept* became a best-selling book.
   I: his last writing assignment at Harvard

   ____

ACTIVITY 64 **Practice Identifying FT, TE, and TI**

Underline the sentence pattern that best describes each sentence below.

From ***Drip! Drop! How Water Gets to Your Tap***
by Barbara Seuling

1.	Water comes in three forms: a liquid, a gas, and a solid.	**FT**	**TE**	**TI**
2.	Water is salty, as in the oceans, or frozen in glaciers.	**FT**	**TE**	**TI**
3.	It doesn't matter how much water evaporates because it always comes back to earth as rain, snow, sleet, or hail.	**FT**	**TE**	**TI**
4.	Large objects are filtered out of water—fish, boots, plastic bags, leaves.	**FT**	**TE**	**TI**
5.	Minerals, such as sulfur, are taken out of water.	**FT**	**TE**	**TI**
6.	It can be a problem if water flows too slowly or too fast.	**FT**	**TE**	**TI**

"The Paddle-Wheel Boat"

7.	More than a hundred years ago, two boys were fishing in a small river.	**FT**	**TE**	**TI**
8.	They sat in a heavy flat-bottomed boat, each holding a fishing rod.	**FT**	**TE**	**TI**
9.	When they wanted to move the boat from one place to another, they had to push against a long pole whose lower end reached the bottom of the river.	**FT**	**TE**	**TI**
10.	The boys needed a lot of time to get anywhere because the boat crept over the water no faster than a snail.	**FT**	**TE**	**TI**
11.	If they wanted to move faster, they had to invent a way.	**FT**	**TE**	**TI**
12.	After a great deal of trying, they did succeed in making two paddle wheels.	**FT**	**TE**	**TI**
13.	They fastened each of these wheels to the end of an iron rod, first passing the rod through the boat from side to side.	**FT**	**TE**	**TI**
14.	They bent the rod in the middle, making a crank for turning.	**FT**	**TE**	**TI**
15.	When the work was finished, the old fishing boat had a paddle wheel on each side which dipped just a few inches into the water.	**FT**	**TE**	**TI**
16.	One of the boys, Robert Fulton, kept on planning and thinking.	**FT**	**TE**	**TI**
17.	We know him as the inventor of the steamboat because he went on to make a paddle boat that could be run by steam.	**FT**	**TE**	**TI**

ACTIVITY 65 **Identifying All Sentence Patterns**

Underline the sentence pattern that best describes each sentence below.

Adapted from: ***Ant Cities***
by Arthur Dorros, pp. 9–22

1. Underneath an ant hill, there may be miles of tunnels and hundreds of rooms.

   T **T,+T** **T=** **LT** **FT** **TE** **TI**

2. It is dark inside the hill, but the ants stay cozy.

   T **T,+T** **T=** **LT** **FT** **TE** **TI**

3. Worker ants do many different kinds of work in the rooms of the hill.

   T **T,+T** **T=** **LT** **FT** **TE** **TI**

4. It is like a city, a busy city of ants.

   T **T,+T** **T=** **LT** **FT** **TE** **TI**

5. In one room of the nest, a queen ant lays eggs.

   T **T,+T** **T=** **LT** **FT** **TE** **TI**

6. Worker ants carry the ants to other rooms and take care of them.

   T **T,+T** **T=** **LT** **FT** **TE** **TI**

7. All of the other ants in the ant city grow from the eggs.

   T **T,+T** **T=** **LT** **FT** **TE** **TI**

8. At first, the tiny eggs grow into larvae.

   T **T,+T** **T=** **LT** **FT** **TE** **TI**

9. The worker ants feed the larvae and lick them clean.

   T **T,+T** **T=** **LT** **FT** **TE** **TI**

10. Harvester ants will bite if you disturb their nest.

    T **T,+T** **T=** **LT** **FT** **TE** **TI**

11. When one ant finds food, the others follow.

    T **T,+T** **T=** **LT** **FT** **TE** **TI**

ACTIVITY 66 Practice Editing for Sentence Patterns III

Errors in sentence patterns below are marked with symbols in the right margin. Correct the sentences based on the symbols and use the symbols to label the sentences.

1. My dad Randy works for the Canadian Forest Department. **TI**

   T I
   My dad, Randy, works for the Canadian Forest Department.

2. Buck is my favorite dog. he works for my dad. he pulls the sleds. **T T T (3 sentences)**

   T T T
   Buck is my favorite dog. He works for my dad. He pulls the sleds.

3. Buck doesn't like to be boss but he is a great leader. **T, +T**

   ____

4. When my dad came back. I was so excited, because I had missed Buck. **FTE (one sentence)**

   ____

5. I played with him all day, and didn't see my mom call me for dinner. **T=**

   ____

6. My favorite building of all is the MSD gym called Benson Gym. Which has a swimming pool, basketball court, and bowling alley. **TI**

   ____

   ____

7. When I was on my way to the field. I heard someone yelling loudly to me. **FT**

   ____

8. Charlie a boy I know is very mischievous, he makes spitballs in class puts thumb tacks under seats puts cherry bombs in the toilets which make horrible sounds. **TI T= =I (two sentences)**

   ____

   ____

   ____

➧ more on next page

9. One day, Charlie was in class he was making spitballs and spit on his teacher. **LT T= (two sentences)**

____

10. The next day the principal went to Charlie's house he saw Charlie and his parents making spitballs on the kitchen table. **LT, +TI (one sentence)**

____

____

ACTIVITY 67 Practice Editing for Sentence Patterns IV

Errors in sentence patterns below are marked with symbols in the right margin. Correct the sentences based on the symbols and use the symbols to label the sentences. The first two are done for you.

1. We visited Rose Hill Manor, we went into a log cabin. **T=**

   T **=**
   We visited Rose Hill Manor and went into a log cabin.

2. In 2050 each MSD student will have two laptops. One will be for school, the other one will be left at home for homework. **FT** **T, +T** **(two sentences)**

   F **T** **T** **, +**
   In 2050, each MSD student will have two laptops. One will be for school, and
   T
   the other one will be left at home for homework.

3. The dog was so thirsty. It went to the toilet for water. **T, +T**

   ____

4. For a few months. She took care of the dog they played a lot and they looked like a cute couple—a dog and an old person. **FT** **T= I** **(two sentences)**

   ____

   ____

5. Because she refused to eat. She started to lose a lot of weight and it made her more depressed. **FT, +T** **(one sentence)**

   ____

   ____

6. He was hoping his father would show up. While he was playing basketball. **TE**

   ____

7. When he arrived home. There was his dad lying down watching TV. **FTI**

   ____

➡ **more on next page**

8. My mother did not work outside the home. When I was growing up. There always was the smell of rice and beans slowly cooking in the kitchen. **T FTI (two sentences)**

____

____

9. She never sat with us, because she preferred to stand and serve us. **TE**

____

10. By the time she was ready to sit down. I had left the kitchen. **FT**

____

ACTIVITY 68 Practice Editing for Sentence Patterns V

Errors in sentence patterns below are marked with symbols in the right margin. Correct the sentences based on the symbols and use the symbols to label the sentences. The first one is done for you.

Adapted from: ***Killing Mr. Griffin***
by Lois Duncan, pp. 8–11

1. For the last year of her life Susan had dreamed about David every night. **FT**

   F **T**
   For the last year of her life, Susan had dreamed about David every night.

2. In some of the dreams he smiled at her, however, in other dreams he didn't notice her. **FT**

   L FT
   (two sentences)

3. Susan took off her glasses, and wiped the dust from them. **T=**

4. David had moved away from her, when she put them on again. **TE**

5. The only handsome boys were the McConnells and most of the time she hated all three of them. **T, +FT**

6. She waited in the classroom doorway looking around the room. **TI**

7. She smiled at two girls but they were talking to each other, and didn't seem to notice her. **T, +T=**

➧ more on next page

 (continued from page 83)

8. She was a straight-A student. As a result, students never asked her about homework. **T LT**

____

____

9. The mid-term exam had been a disaster for everyone, or the final was going to be even harder. **T, +T**

____

____

10. They thought that Mr. Griffin their teacher was too hard a teacher. **TI**

____

Section 4

• Boxes and Main Words
• Countable and Uncountable Boxes
• *THE* Boxes
• Referents
• Editing Practice

Key teaching points:

Main words (nouns) live in boxes.

They can show one or many and can be replaced with referents.

ACTIVITY 69 **Boxes and Main Words**

Boxes are places where nouns live with other words that work for them. They are also places where words like *it, they, he, she, them* can substitute for nouns. Boxes can be found before the verb—in subject position (do you remember how to find the subject of a sentence?), or after the verb. Every box must have at least one noun (or its substitute) and that noun (or its substitute) is the *main word* of the box. It tells us what the box is really about. An asterisk (*) is above the main words in the boxes below.

Adapted from ***The Magic School Bus Inside the Human Body***
by Joanna Cole and Bruce Degen, pp. 6–26

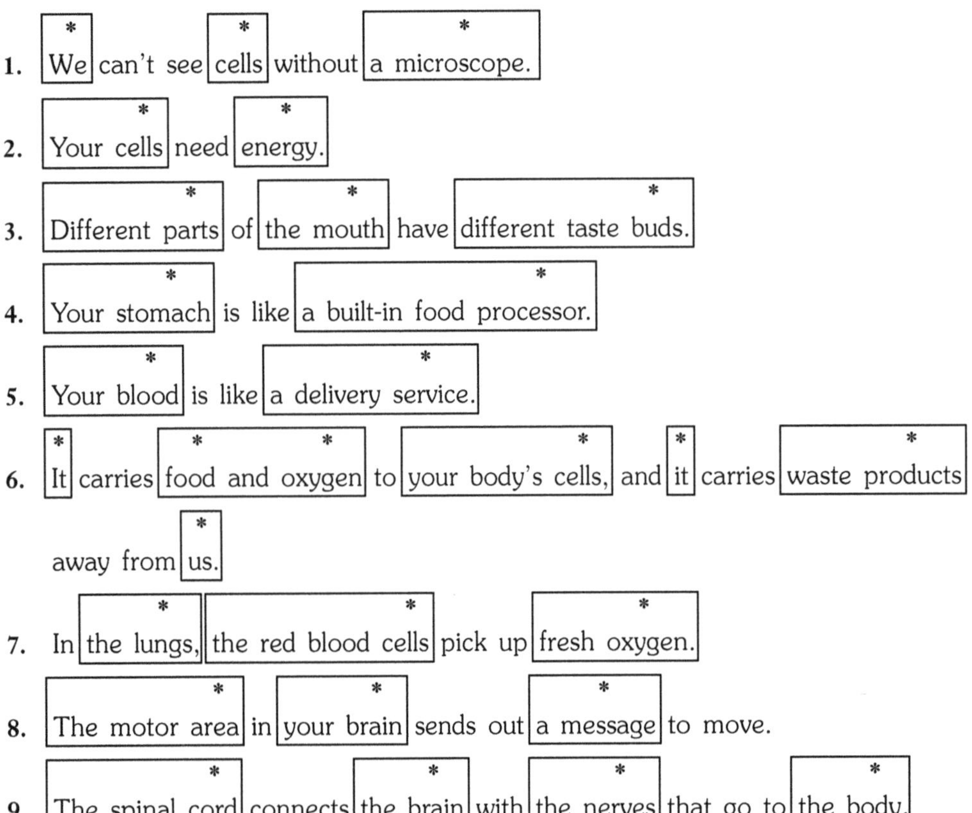

1. We can't see cells without a microscope.
2. Your cells need energy.
3. Different parts of the mouth have different taste buds.
4. Your stomach is like a built-in food processor.
5. Your blood is like a delivery service.
6. It carries food and oxygen to your body's cells, and it carries waste products away from us.
7. In the lungs, the red blood cells pick up fresh oxygen.
8. The motor area in your brain sends out a message to move.
9. The spinal cord connects the brain with the nerves that go to the body.

ACTIVITY 70 **Practice with Boxes**

Place an asterisk (*) over the main words in the boxes below.

Adapted from **"Good Earth"** in ***New Practice Readers***
by Anderson, Stone, and Burton, p. 136

1. [The earth*] is covered with [soil.*]

2. [Most soil] is made of [ground-up bits] of [rocks.]

3. [Rocks] mix with [dead leaves,] [parts] of [dead plants, and dead animals,] too.

4. [All these things,] mixing together for [a long, long, time,] make [soil.]

Now . . . find the boxes in the following sentences and place an asterisk above the main words in them.

Adapted from ***From Plants to Blue Jeans***
by L'Hommedieu, pp. 4–11

1. [Blue jeans*] were invented by [Levi Strauss.*]

2. These tough pants have been worn by all sorts of people.

3. Blue jeans begin on a cotton farm.

4. Special machines plant cotton seeds in many rows.

5. Small white flowers form on the little cotton plants.

6. The flowers change color and die.

7. They leave tiny pods.

8. The pods are called cotton bolls.

ACTIVITY 71 **More Practice with Boxes**

Find the boxes in the following sentences and place an asterisk (*) above the main word or words in them.

"The Year Is 1902"

From: www.goofball.com/jokes/facts/2003016101

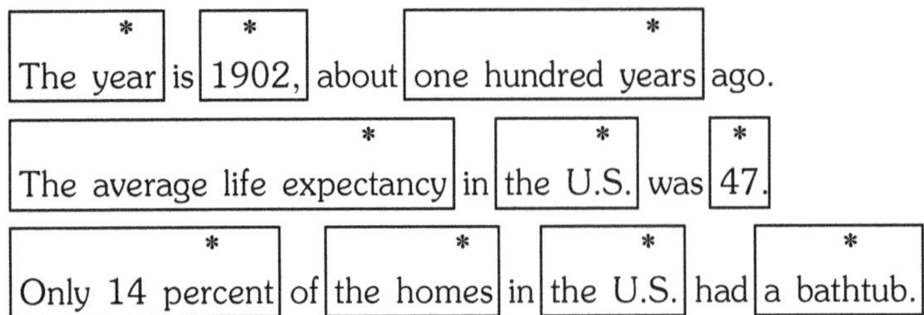

Only 8 percent of the homes had a telephone.

A three-minute call from Denver to New York City cost 11 dollars.

There were only 8,000 cars in the U.S. and only 144 miles of paved roads.

The maximum speed limit in most cities was 10 mph.

Alabama, Mississippi, Iowa, and Tennessee were each more heavily populated than California.

The tallest structure in the world was the Eiffel Tower.

The average wage in the U.S. was 22 cents an hour.

The average U.S. worker made between $200 and $400 per year.

A competent accountant could expect to earn $2,000 per year. Sugar cost 4 cents a pound.

Most women only washed their hair once a month and used borax or egg yolks for shampoo.

The five leading causes of death in the U.S. were: pneumonia and influenza,

tuberculosis, diarrhea, heart disease, and stroke.

The American flag had 45 stars. Arizona, Oklahoma, New Mexico, Hawaii, and Alaska

hadn't been admitted to the Union yet.

The population of Las Vegas, Nevada, was 30.

Crossword puzzles, canned beer, and iced tea hadn't been invented.

ACTIVITY 72 **Focusing on Nouns**

Study the nouns on the left and the nouns on the right, then answer the questions at the bottom of the page.

suitcase/bag/trunk a another each	luggage
suitcases/bags/trunks 2, 3, 4 . . . many	
coin/bill/check/quarter a another each	money
coins/bills/checks/quarters 2, 3, 4 . . . many	
sofa/lamp/chair/table a another each	furniture
sofas/lamps/chairs/tables 2, 3, 4 . . . many	
bat/racket/base/glove a another each	equipment
bats/rackets/bases/gloves 2, 3, 4 . . . many	

➡ Can you show one or many of the nouns on the left? YES NO

Can you show one or many of the nouns on the right? YES NO

ACTIVITY 73 Countable and Uncountable Boxes

Boxes that show one and many are called *countable boxes*. Some ways to show one or many are to use words such as *a, an, another, each, many* and to use *numbers*. You can also add an *s*. Boxes that do not show one or many are called *uncountable boxes*. See Appendix F for nouns/boxes that can be both countable and uncountable as well as some other uncountable nouns/boxes. If you want to know if a noun is countable or uncountable, check a dictionary. In most learner's dictionaries of American English, uncountable nouns will be labeled like this: spaghetti, n. [U].

Study the boxes on the left to see how the main words inside them show one or many. Study the boxes on the right to see how the main words do not show one or many. Read across.

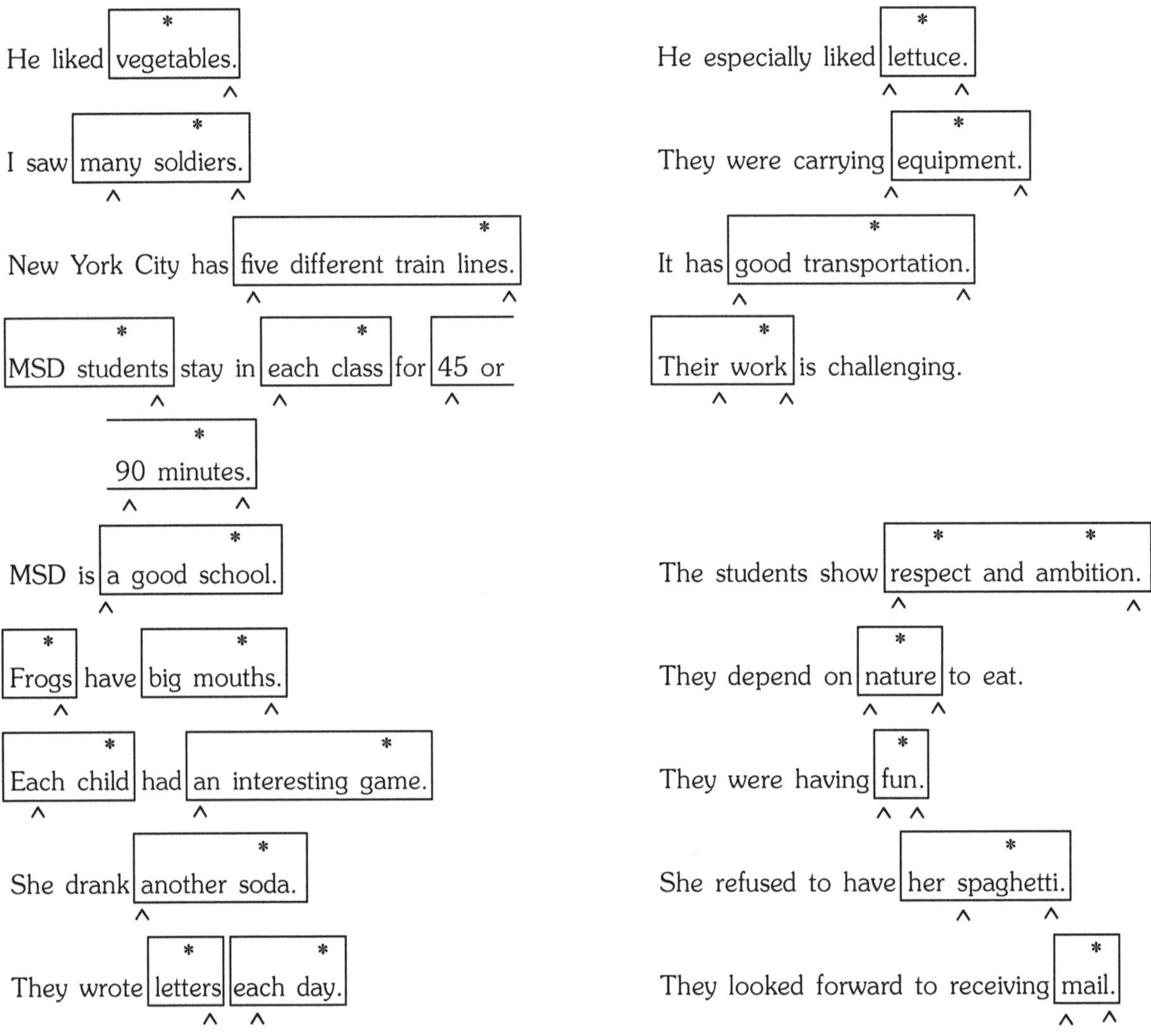

ACTIVITY 74 **Practice with Countable and Uncountable Boxes**

In the boxes below, place an asterisk over the main words and ^ to the left or right of the main words to show one or many if the main words are countable. If the main words are uncountable, place a *u* inside the box. Use activities 72 and 73 and Appendix F to help you.

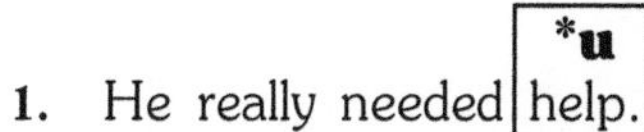

1. He really needed help.

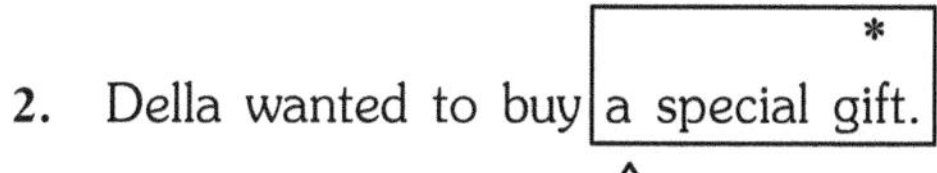

2. Della wanted to buy a special gift.

3. His friends live far away.

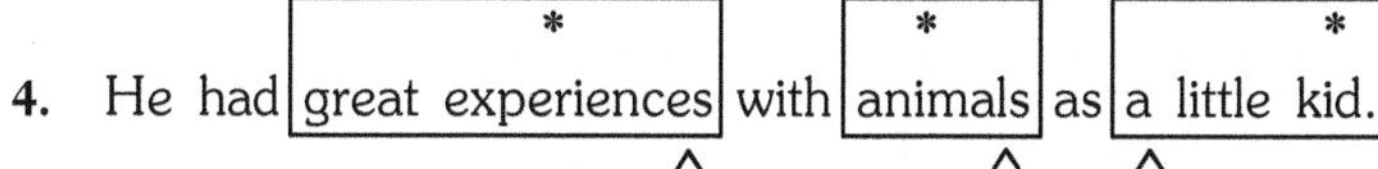

4. He had great experiences with animals as a little kid.

5. I prefer to eat healthfully and not take medicine.

6. She gave incorrect information to her friends.

7. For her birthday, she got a chocolate Labrador retriever.

8. She writes in two diaries each night.

9. Some houses need fresh air.

10. They looked like a cute couple.

11. Gino would never leave her for another girl.

12. Joshua ran to get dog medicine.

ACTIVITY 75 Practice Correcting Countable and Uncountable Errors

In the boxes below, use ^ to show errors and then correct them. Write a small *u* above uncountable errors and correct them as well. Use activities 72–73 and Appendix F to help you.

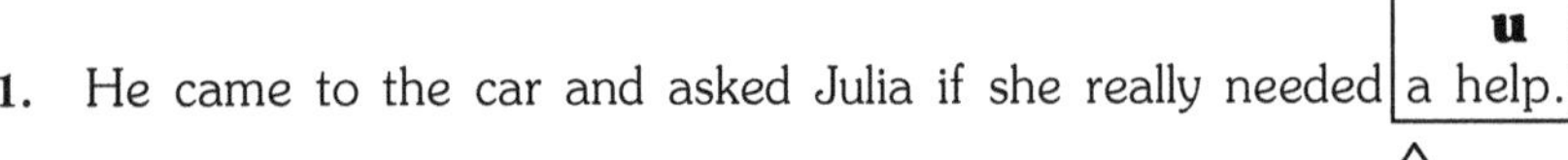

1. He came to the car and asked Julia if she really needed a help.

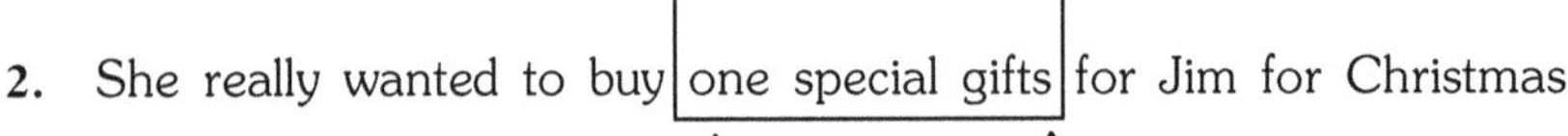

2. She really wanted to buy one special gifts for Jim for Christmas.

3. Her internship experience gave her a wonderful opportunities.

4. The little girl had many piece of chalks.

5. They will allow Joshua to get another dogs.

6. NYC has good transportations.

7. I saw a small bowl. It was made with woods.

8. There aren't many tree near the beach.

9. Their homeworks is always done well.

ACTIVITY 76 ***THE* Boxes**

Writers use THE to show readers special things or things readers already know about. Readers might know about them because:

1. There is only one in the world.

   The sun . . . the moon . . . the Gulf of Mexico . . . the Bahamas . . .
   the Atlantic . . . the United States of America . . . the Titanic . . .
   the *Frederick Post*

2. They are made special by what follows them.

The player who finishes first will win.	(not just any player)
Please give me *the cup that is broken*.	(not just any cup)

3. They refer back to something already mentioned.

   Mr. Frappa, who owned *a grocery store* on Maple Avenue, kept
   a large black book with the names of people who owed him money.
   When I walked in *the store*, I could see *the book*.
   (Adapted from De Young 1999, p.7)

4. There is only one in the environment you are in or can assume there's one in the environment you are reading about.

Let's go to *the library*.	(Students are at school.)
Isn't *the park* beautiful!	(People are in a park.)
When I walked in, I could see it on *the counter*.	(A person was in a place with one counter.)

5. Writers/speakers assume you already know what they are talking about outside the environment.

Wasn't *the dress* perfect for her?	(Friends had already seen a dress.)
The President's plan is good.	(People learned about the plan before.)
What did you think of *the movie*?	(Friends saw a movie.)
Let's go to *the movies*.	(People know what movies are.)

ACTIVITY 77 Recognizing Reasons for *THE* Boxes

Why does the author C. Coco De Young use *the* the way she does in the following passages from *A Letter to Mrs. Roosevelt* (pp. 6–7)? The numbers above the words *the* below refer to the reasons described in activity 76. Do you agree?

Papa owned a shoe repair shop on Bedford Street. I often walked to work with him when there was no school. Every morning at six o'clock he crossed over the[1] First Street Bridge, stopped to greet Mr. Bobb, who operated the[2] train tower on the[3] bridge, then walked the[2] long trek past the[4] steel mill. Papa stopped whistling and tipped his hat in respect as he passed St. John's Church. At the[2] corner near the[1] Swank Building, he started to whistle again, and continued until he reached the[3] shop. As Papa unlocked the[4] door, he would pause to breathe in the[2] balmy scents of leather and shoe polish. Then he'd turn on the[4] lights, walk behind the[4] counter, and put on his apron.

In the[5] late afternoon, Papa closed the[3] shop and walked past the[2] bank on Main Street. There was a time when he would stop in the[3] bank every Friday, just before closing. That was when he carried a small sack of money, proof of a busy week. He would smile as he proudly handed the[3] sack over to the[2] teller behind the[4] counter. Sometimes Mr. Lockhard, the[3] bank president, would smile back and shake Papa's hand. Not anymore. Now Papa walked by the[3] bank jingling the[2] small change in his pocket, sometimes carrying a basket of fresh fruit and vegetables.

Today I heard him tell Mama that Mr. Lockhard stood in the[2] window of the[3] bank yesterday. Papa tipped his hat, but Mr. Lockhard didn't seem to notice as he stared out at Main Street. He stopped shaking Papa's hand a long time ago, when Papa stopped carrying the[3] money sack. Now Papa used the[3] pocket change to pay our food bill.

ACTIVITY 78 **Practice with *THE* Boxes #1**

Draw a box around the *the* boxes below and write a number over the *the* word to show the reason for its use. Use activity 76 to help.

Adapted from **"Freedom"** in ***Wayside School Is Falling Down***
by Louis Sachar, pp. 36–37

Myron crumbled a cracker on [**2** the windowsill] next to his desk, then looked away. He knew Oddly came only when nobody was looking.

A little while later a bird landed on the windowsill and ate the crumbs. Myron watched him out of the corner of his eye.

He was a black bird with a pink breast. Myron had named him "Oddly."

"Is that your dumb bird again?" asked Kathy.

"No," said Myron. "Oddly is not *my* bird. I don't own him. He doesn't live in a cage. Oddly is free!"

"You're a birdbrain," said Kathy.

Myron watched Oddly fly away. He wished he could fly away across the sky with Oddly.

Oddly probably thinks I live in a cage, he realized. Whenever he sees me, I'm sitting in this same desk. He probably thinks this desk is my cage!

So Myron got out of his chair and sat on the floor.

"Myron, what are you doing out of your seat?" asked Mrs. Jewls.

"I want to sit on the floor," said Myron.

"Get back to your seat," ordered Mrs. Jewls.

I *do* live in a cage, he thought. And I have to stay in the cage until the bell rings!

ACTIVITY 79 **Practice with *THE* Boxes #2**

Draw a box around the *the* boxes below and write a number over the *the* word to show the reason for its use. Use activity 76 to help.

"Two Great Painters"

There was once a painter whose name was Zeuxis, and he could paint pictures so life-like that they were mistaken for [**2** the real things] which they represented. At one time, he painted the picture of some fruit which was so real that birds flew down and pecked at it. This made him very proud of his skill.

"I am the only man in the world who can paint a picture so true to life," he said.

There was another famous artist whose name was Parrhasius. When he heard of the boast which Zeuxis had made, he said to himself, "I will see what I can do."

So he painted a beautiful picture which seemed to be covered with a curtain. Then he invited Zeuxis to come and see it.

Zeuxis looked at it closely. "Pull the curtain aside and show us the picture," he said.

Parrhasius laughed and answered, "The curtain is the picture."

"Well," said Zeuxis, "you have beaten me this time, and I shall boast no more. I deceived only the birds, but you have deceived me, a painter."

Some time after this, Zeuxis painted another wonderful picture. It was that of a boy carrying a basket of ripe red cherries. When he hung this painting outside his door, some birds flew down and tried to carry the cherries away.

"Ah! This picture is a failure," he said. "If the boy had been as well painted as the cherries, the birds would have been afraid to come near him."

ACTIVITY 80 Practice with *THE* Boxes #3

Draw a box around the *the* boxes below and write a number over the *the* word to show the reason for its use. Use activity 76 to help.

From **"Splendor"** in ***Reading Fluency, Level C***
by Lois Lowry, p. 29

To Becky's surprise, her mother smiled. "You have your baby-sitting money in [**5** the bank,] Beck," she said. "And it's your very first real dance. If you want to spend that much on a special dress—well, it's up to you."

"Mom," said Angela, "nobody dances with seventh graders anyway. The seventh-grade boys won't dance. They all stand around in the corners with each other. And the eighth-grade boys only dance with the eighth-grade girls. So what's the point of spending all your money on a dress if no one's going to dance with you? I *told* Becky she could wear my blue dress to the dance. The one I wore last year."

"I don't want to wear a hand-me-down dress, not to the Christmas dance," Becky exploded. "*You* didn't have to wear someone else's dress when you were in seventh grade!"

"Becky," Angela pointed out in her logical, patronizing way, "I didn't have an older sister. So who could hand a dress down?"

"It's not my fault I was born second."

"Shhh," said their mother. "Calm down. You buy the dress, honey, if it's what you want. It's important to have a very special dress now and then."

ACTIVITY 81 **Referents**

Referents are words that replace or refer to boxes. This way, you do not have to keep repeating the boxes themselves. Words like *he/him*, *she/her*, *they/them* and *it* are referents. They are also called *pronouns*. In the passage below, *Ref* is written above the referents. Draw arrows from these referents to the boxes they replace or refer to.

From ***The Ways of Written English***
by Louis Inturrisi, p. 114

Ref **Ref**
Donald Thornton is a 52-year-old black man, a widower and a janitor. He has six daughters. And he

Ref **Ref** **Ref**
had a dream for them. He wished that someday, they would all become doctors. Things did not work

Ref **Ref**
out exactly according to Mr. Thornton's dream, but they came close, so that today he is a happy man.

Ref
Mr. Thornton says he doesn't know a whole lot about Women's Lib, but even as a young boy

Ref **Ref**
he sensed that "girls were taken advantage of by boys" and that they should be "put in a place where

Ref
they don't have to take no junk from boys." So when Donald and his wife began raising their girls,

Ref **Ref** **Ref** **Ref***
they vowed to "make them so strong that nobody could hurt them." It was Mr. Thornton's idea to

Ref **Ref**
make his daughters doctors, but he worried about how to put them through college on a

Ref
janitor's salary. One day the answer came in the bottom of a Cracker Jack box. It was a tiny plastic

Ref
saxophone. Donnalee, the youngest of Mr. Thornton's daughters, fell in love with it, even though

Ref
it was no bigger than her hand.

That Christmas Donnalee was given a real saxophone. Then Jeannette, the second child, had to

Ref
have a guitar. Then came Betty who wasn't musical, so she got a tambourine. Yvonne was next.

Ref
She played the alto sax. Then Linda took up the drums. Rita, the last girl, learned the piano.

Ref
Soon all six girls began to play together as a group. They called themselves "The Thornton Sisters."

The group soon managed to get itself into show business. As a result of their success, the Thorntons

were able to save enough money to finance their children's education.

➡ **more on next page**

ACTIVITY 81 *(continued from page 98)*

So far there are three "Drs. Thornton." All three have promised their father to use their maiden

Ref

name professionally to show respect for him. The other three daughters are now in medical school pursuing their studies.

ACTIVITY 82 Understanding Different Forms of Referents

Referents that refer to the same box can be spelled differently. List all the boxes on the left from the story about the Thornton Sisters (activity 81) and then all their referents on the right, in the correct column. The first few are done for you.

	Referents	
Boxes	***Before The Verb***	***After The Verb***
Donald Thornton (Mr. Thornton)	he	
six daughters	they	them
Things	they	

Which referents come before the verb? ________, ________, ________, ________

Which referents come after the verb? ________, ________, ________

ACTIVITY 83 Choosing the Correct Referent

In the passage below, choose the correct referent in parentheses so that it matches its box and write *Ref* above the correct referent. Draw a box around its box and an arrow from the referent to its box. The first one is done for you.

Adapted from **"The Gossiper"** in ***Chicken Soup for the Teenage Soul***
by Cannfield, Hansen, and Kirberger, pp. 41–42

A woman repeated a bit of gossip about a neighbor. Within a few days the whole community knew the story. The neighbor was deeply hurt. Later, the woman responsible for spreading the gossip learned that (it/she) was not true. (She/He) was very sorry and went to a wise old sage to find out what (she/he) could do to stop the gossip.

Ref

"Go to the marketplace," (he/him) said, "and purchase a chicken, and have (it/him) killed. Then on your way home, pluck its feathers and drop (it/them) one by one along the road." Although surprised by this advice, the woman did what (he/it) said.

The next day the wise man said, "Now, go and collect all those feathers you dropped yesterday and bring (it/them) back to me."

The woman followed the same road, but to her dismay the wind had blown all the feathers away. After searching for hours, (they/she) returned with only three in her hand. "You see," said the sage, "it's easy to drop (it/them), but it's impossible to get (it/them) back. So it is with gossip. It doesn't take much to spread gossip, but once you do, you can never take (it/them) back."

ACTIVITY 84 More Practice with Referents

Write *Ref* above the incorrectly matched referent in the sentences below. Draw a box around its box and put an asterisk over the main word in the box. Draw an arrow from the referent to its box. Then, correct the referent. The first one is done for you.

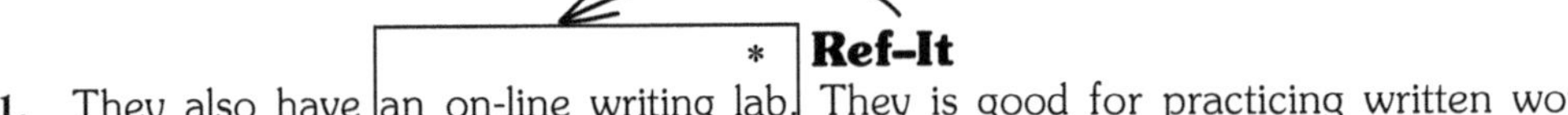

Ref–It

1. They also have an on-line writing lab. They is good for practicing written work.

2. The ants create houses underground. It are called colonies.

3. The airport builders agreed to have sidewalks that can move by itself.

4. When ants are hungry, them use antennae to smell and find food. Antennae are on their heads.

5. The park has lots of trees. Also they has a lot of land with grass.

6. I got here and pulled out many flowers. I took them to my home and gave it to my mom.

7. She always hated her freckles while I always thought it were so cute.

8. Then the man came back from where he was, and I decided to follow her.

In the sentences below, boxes are repeated. Write *Ref?* above the repeated box and correct it with an appropriate referent. The first one is done for you.

Ref?–it

9. I grabbed the flag and waved the flag.

10. The dog was so thirsty. The dog showed its thirsty face.

11. Tarlie realized that Gino, the dog, was very loyal to her. Gino always slept with Tarlie.

12. Jerry thinks that he might need to spend more time with the hamster to appreciate what his sister sees in the hamster.

13. Classes will be canceled tomorrow because tomorrow is a holiday.

14. Leave the books outside my office. Someone will come to pick the books up later.

ACTIVITY 85 Practice Editing Inside Boxes and for Referents I

Edit the following sentences using the correction symbol or symbols inside each sentence to help you find the errors. The first one is done for you.

Adapted from **"Secrets from the Desert"** in ***Reading Fluency, Level C***
by Camille L. Z. Blachowicz, p. 22

1. It all started with a goat. At least, that's the way the story goes.

   1 the
2. The story comes from a shepherd boy in Middle East.

3. This boys^ lived in Jordan. One day, in 1947, he and his goats were out in the desert,

   1
   near Dead Sea.

   3
4. One of the goats ran off. The boy saw it go into a cave. He threw a stones^ into a cave to scare the goat out.

   Ref
5. When the stone landed, the boy heard something break.

   3
6. The boy ran off and brought a friend back to cave.

   Ref 3
7. Together he climbed into dark, dry cave.

   3
8. There they saw what a stone had hit.

9. Lying on the floor were some old pottery jar^.

   Ref
10. These jar^ weren't just old—it were ancient. They were 2,000 year^ old.

11. Rolled up in the jars were some old paper^ as old as the jars. The boy^ did not know it then,

    Ref 2 3
    but the paper^ were of great importance. It were first part of Dead Sea Scrolls.

12. Researcher^ and scientist^ call the Dead Sea Scrolls one of the greatest finds ever.

ACTIVITY 86 **Practice Editing Inside Boxes and for Referents II**

Edit the following sentences using the correction symbol or symbols inside each sentence to help you find the errors. The first one is done for you.

Adapted from **"Women at War"** in ***Reading Fluency, Level D***
by Camille L. Z. Blachowicz, p. 9

1. Between 1961 and 1973, more than 7,000 military women served in Vietnam.

2. At that time, women were not trained for fighting. Most were nurse.
   ^

3. Many served in hospital that were located near the action.
   ^

   u
4. Army nurses had to deal with their patients' pain and sufferings.
   ^

   u
5. Some soldier, as a result of their wounds, would be crippled for lifes.
   ^ ^

   2 **2**
6. Often last face that a dying soldiers saw was face of a nurses.
   ^ ^ ^ ^

7. Connie Curtley was a nurse in Vietnam. Her many memory of the wars are painful.
   ^ ^

   Ref **Ref**
8. They describes the smell of the dirty uniforms that they cut off the wounded men.

   u
9. At times, Curtley treated so many wounded man that her own cloth were soaked in bloods.
   ^ ^

   Ref
10. Curtley said her uniform was so full of dried blood, they was hard.

    3
11. Year after a war, nurses still have trouble shaking these memories.
    ^

Appendices

Appendix A
X-Words: Before and Now

Before	At some time before . . . maybe continuing into now	Now
did		does do
had	has have	
would could should might		will/would can/could shall/should may/might must
was were		is are am

Appendix B

X-Words: 1 or 2 or Many

1	**2 or Many**
i*s*	are
wa*s*	were
ha*s*	have
doe*s*	do
will/would can/could shall/should may/might/must	will/would can/could shall/should may/might/must
had	had
did	did

Appendix C

Some Main Verb Forms

With X-Words That Show			With X-Words That Hide		
		(Time and how many are in the X-words)			
BASE	***ING***	***D-T-N***	**V/XS**	**V/XO**	**V/XD**
do, does, did will, would can, could shall, should may, might, must	is, am, are, was, were	has, have, had	(hidden *does*)	(hidden *do*)	(hidden *did*)
abandon	abandoning	abandoned	abandons	abandon	abandoned
accept	accepting	accepted	accepts	accept	accepted
allow	allowing	allowed	allows	allow	allowed
ask	asking	asked	asks	ask	asked
bark	barking	barked	barks	bark	barked
be	being	been	—	—	—
bother	bothering	bothered	bothers	bother	bothered
call	calling	called	calls	call	called
change	changing	changed	changes	change	changed
choose	choosing	chosen	chooses	choose	chose
come	coming	come	comes	come	came
consider	considering	considered	considers	consider	considered
convince	convincing	convinced	convinces	convince	convinced
deserve	deserving	deserved	deserves	deserve	deserved
destroy	destroying	destroyed	destroys	destroy	destroyed
die	dying	died	dies	die	died
distract	distracting	distracted	distracts	distract	distracted
do	doing	done	does	do	did
doubt	doubting	doubted	doubts	doubt	doubted
drive	driving	driven	drives	drive	drove
expect	expecting	expected	expects	expect	expected
feel	feeling	felt	feels	feel	felt
fight	fighting	fought	fights	fight	fought
find	finding	found	finds	find	found

With X-Words That Show			With X-Words That Hide		
		(Time and how many are in the X-words)			
BASE	***ING***	***D-T-N***	**V/XS**	**V/XO**	**V/XD**
do, does, did will, would can, could shall, should may, might, must	is, am, are, was, were	has, have, had	(hidden *does*)	(hidden *do*)	(hidden *did*)
fix	fixing	fixed	fixes	fix	fixed
get	getting	gotten	gets	get	got
give	giving	given	gives	give	gave
go	going	gone	goes	go	went
grieve	grieving	grieved	grieves	grieve	grieved
guide	guiding	guided	guides	guide	guided
have	having	had	has	have	had
hate	hating	hated	hates	hate	hated
hear	hearing	heard	hears	hear	heard
invent	inventing	invented	invents	invent	invented
interrupt	interrupting	interrupted	interrupts	interrupt	interrupted
kill	killing	killed	kills	kill	killed
know	knowing	known	knows	know	knew
leave	leaving	left	leaves	leave	left
let	letting	let	lets	let	let
live	living	lived	lives	live	lived
look	looking	looked	looks	look	looked
lose	losing	lost	loses	lose	lost
make	making	made	makes	make	made
marry	marrying	married	marries	marry	married
meet	meeting	met	meets	meet	met
mention	mentioning	mentioned	mentions	mention	mentioned
motivate	motivating	motivated	motivates	motivate	motivated
obey	obeying	obeyed	obeys	obey	obeyed
pay	paying	paid	pays	pay	paid
polish	polishing	polished	polishes	polish	polished
put (on)	putting (on)	put (on)	puts (on)	put (on)	put (on)
raise	raising	raised	raises	raise	raised

With X-Words That Show			**With X-Words That Hide**		
(Time and how many are in the X-words)					
BASE	***ING***	***D-T-N***	**V/XS**	**V/XO**	**V/XD**
do, does, did will, would can, could shall, should may, might, must	is, am, are, was, were	has, have, had	(hidden *does*)	(hidden *do*)	(hidden *did*)
reach	reaching	reached	reaches	reach	reached
read	reading	read	reads	read	read
relieve	relieving	relieved	relieves	relieve	relieved
ride	riding	ridden	rides	ride	rode
rise	rising	risen	rises	rise	rose
say	saying	said	says	say	said
see	seeing	seen	sees	see	saw
seem	seeming	seemed	seems	seem	seemed
send	sending	sent	sends	send	sent
stand	standing	stood	stands	stand	stood
stop	stopping	stopped	stops	stop	stopped
take	taking	taken	takes	take	took
think	thinking	thought	thinks	think	thought
try	trying	tried	tries	try	tried
understand	understanding	understood	understands	understand	understood
walk	walking	walked	walks	walk	walked
want	wanting	wanted	wants	want	wanted

Appendix D

Linkers

"Sequence in Time" Linkers

Finally,
The next day,
First, Second, etc.
Then
Later (on),
Meanwhile,
At the same time,
Now,

"And" Linkers

In addition,
Also,

"But" Linkers

However,
Still,
Instead,

"So" Linkers

As a result,
Therefore,

"Different Way" Linkers

On the other hand,

"Explanation" Linkers

In other words,
For example,
For instance,

"Detail" Linkers

In fact,
Actually,

Appendix E
Common Shifter Words and Phrases

Time Shifters

Before school, I called my mother.

After school, I called my mother.

During school, I called my mother.

When school started, I called my mother.

At 12 PM, I called my mother.

Last night, I called my mother.

Everyday, I call my mother.

A few days ago, I called my mother.

In a couple of days, I will call my mother.

Next week, I will call my mother.

While I was eating, I called my mother.

Reason Shifters

Since he was sick, he left school.

Because he was sick, he left school.

Contrast Shifters

Although he was sick, he came to school.

Even though he was sick, he came to school.

Though he was sick, he came to school.

Condition Shifters

If it rains, we won't have a picnic.

Even if it rains, we will have a picnic.

Unless it rains, we will have a picnic.

Where Shifters

Underneath an ant hill, there can be miles of tunnels.

About three feet from us, the bear stood straight up on its back legs.

Appendix F

Countable and Uncountable Nouns/Boxes

Some nouns can be both countable and uncountable depending on the meaning intended.

Countable

(Here the meaning is about specific times or things.)

*
We had a good time.

*
The young wife bought a cooked chicken for dinner.

*
May I take a chocolate?

*
The rich man has three homes.

*
The old man had a long and healthy life.

Uncountable

(Here the meaning is "in general.")

*
Good students use time well.

*
I eat only chicken.

*
Chocolate is made with milk.

*
The college student left home.

*
Live life to the fullest everyday!

Some Other Uncountable Nouns

spaghetti, pollution, tennis,

ice, gold, dirt, anger, happiness,

salt, courage, snow, electricity,

violence, patience, sunshine,

garbage, homework, clothing,

peace, work, vocabulary, news

Appendix G

X -Word Grammar Correction Symbols

Symbol	Meaning	Example
X?	missing X-word	**X?** I ^ getting a light blue scooter on Friday.
~~X~~	too many X-words	All the windows are ~~is~~ very strong.
	unnecessary X-word	I ~~were~~ enjoyed this trip a lot.
WX	wrong X-word	Why **WX** does she sick?
TIME	wrong time reference	How do **Time** you tell your Mom that soldiers had stopped you . . .?
S X	wrong match-up of subject and X-word	[Many dogs] **S** does **X** obey him. He's a leader.
X V	wrong match-up of X-word and main verb	And she saw Shira was **X** rocked **V** outside. And she was **X** watched **V** and waiting for Jessy.
V/X	wrong form of a hidden X-word (hidden *does*)	He does work for my dad. He just **V/XS** pull the sled like other dogs.
	(hidden *do*)	**V/XO** I felt much better right now.
	(hidden *did*)	Jerry brought the hamster home and **V/XD** shows it to his parents.
INF	wrong form of infinitive	I'm beginning (to thinking) **Inf** of a better gift.
T, + T	missing joiner and/or comma	It **T** rained. **,+** The picnic **T** ended.

This appendix is adapted from Kurz and Glock 2000.

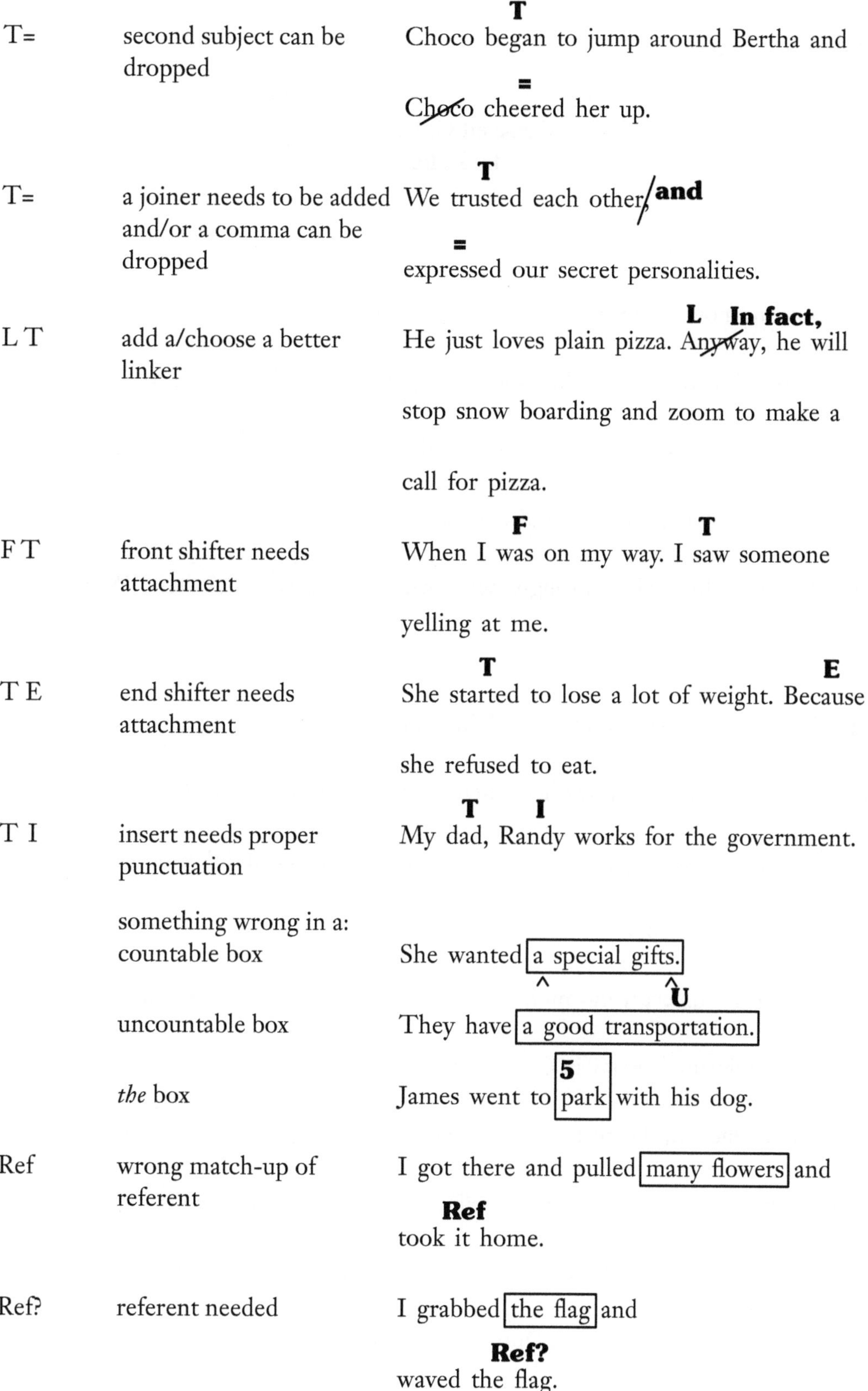

T=	second subject can be dropped	Choco began to jump around Bertha and ~~Choco~~ cheered her up. (marked **T** … **=**)
T=	a joiner needs to be added and/or a comma can be dropped	We trusted each other, **and** expressed our secret personalities. (marked **T** … **=**)
L T	add a/choose a better linker	He just loves plain pizza. ~~Anyway~~ **In fact,** he will stop snow boarding and zoom to make a call for pizza. (marked **L**)
F T	front shifter needs attachment	When I was on my way. I saw someone yelling at me. (marked **F** … **T**)
T E	end shifter needs attachment	She started to lose a lot of weight. Because she refused to eat. (marked **T** … **E**)
T I	insert needs proper punctuation	My dad, Randy works for the government. (marked **T** … **I**)
	something wrong in a: countable box	She wanted [a special gifts.]
	uncountable box	They have [a good transportation.] (marked **U**)
	the box	James went to [park] with his dog. (marked **5**)
Ref	wrong match-up of referent	I got there and pulled [many flowers] and **Ref** took it home.
Ref?	referent needed	I grabbed [the flag] and **Ref?** waved the flag.

Appendix H
Model Essays

Crossed Cultures
by Luke

In the story "Mrs. Dutta Writes a Letter" by Chitra Divakaruni, Mrs. Dutta, an Indian woman, moves from Calcutta, India, to San Francisco, California. She moves to America to live with her son, Sagar, and his family after a long illness. After several months in her new country and home, Mrs. Dutta decides to move back to Calcutta due to the cultural conflict that existed between her and her daughter-in-law, Shyamoli. I strongly agree with the decision that Mrs. Dutta made to go back to her country.

Mrs. Dutta wanted to spend time with her family because she desperately missed her son Sagar and was thrilled when she actually moved in with him. She thought things would go well when she moved in, but she didn't expect that things were going to happen so differently. For example, Mrs. Dutta, at an early age, learned to get up every morning at 5 a.m. to make tea for her husband and family, but during her stay in California, it seems that Sagar doesn't respect this tradition. One day, she mistakenly dropped the alarm clock when she just wanted to make tea for everyone. Sagar tells her "Mother, please don't get up so early in the morning. All that noise in the bathroom, it wakes us up, and Molli has such a long day at work." Mrs. Dutta did not feel appreciated and felt upset after Sagar's statement. Her cultural beliefs and traditions are getting in the way of her ability to get along with and be a part of her family.

Mrs. Dutta was very surprised after she saw her grandchildren react to their parents and to Mrs. Dutta herself. For instance, Mrs. Dutta was in the bathroom and Shyamoli told her daughter, Mrinalini, to use the bathroom downstairs and Mrinalini's reaction was "it's not fair, why can't she go downstairs." After Mrs. Dutta heard what her grandchild said, she felt badly about the way her grandchildren talk to their parents. She feels it's too Americanized, and that they don't have respect for their elders. Mrs. Dutta was also surprised that Shyamoli, as a mother, did not discipline her children for being so disrespectful.

Mrs. Dutta is forcing herself to be happy, but she's living a lie. She gets a letter from her best friend from Calcutta asking her how everything is in California with her son, Sagar. Mrs. Dutta wants to write back but doesn't want to be very negative about her experience because she doesn't want people in her country to know that she is ashamed of how Shyamoli and Sagar are acting; she doesn't want others to know the truth about what happened and how she is feeling. She is unable to express what is really happening in America even to her best friend, and that, I think, is bad. She is going against herself by trying to make things sound better than they are. If she were to go back home, she could again be herself. She wouldn't have to try to blend in while going against all of her own beliefs. In America, she is acting opposite of who she really is.

If Sagar and Shyamoli had known that Mrs. Dutta was unhappy, I think they still wouldn't change their behavior. Shyamoli, as a daughter-in-law, is too embarrassed to hang her clothes outside, as preferred by Mrs. Dutta, because she doesn't want her neighbors to look down at her and think that they are deprived and can't afford to buy a dryer. It seems that Mrs. Dutta can't possibly do anything there to help or be valued enough as a grandmother and a mother to her family because they will not allow her to be herself. She always wanted to come and spend time with her family and always pictured that everything would be perfect. The picture that hung in her bedroom in Calcutta allowed her to fantasize about her family and what it would be like when she came to America, but everything was completely different the moment she arrived. Maybe it would be good for Sagar and Shyamoli to visit Mrs. Dutta in India for them to see and understand their culture.

Abel's Misfortune
by Molly

In the first chapter of *In This Sign* by Joanne Greenberg, the main character of the novel, Abel, is heading for a life of debt. Once after work, on the way home, a car in a showroom of cars caught his attention. Standing for a while, he admired the beautiful cars. The car salesman in the showroom invited Abel to come in and started to advertise with a lot of talk how good the car is. So the salesman, Dengel, convinced Abel to buy the car. Abel did not realize that he only put down a small payment for the car and ignored requests for monthly payments which came by mail. I think that Abel and Dengel were both to blame for Abel's life of debt.

Abel is guilty. When Dengel was speaking to him about the car, Abel pretended to understand. "He didn't need to hear the words to feel the honor, so he smiled and nodded to show how glad he was because of it." Dengel continued to convince Abel to buy the car and Abel "nodded yes, and yes again." I understand Abel's behaviors; he wants to feel respected as he said, ". . . he called me 'sir.'" He didn't want Dengel to find out that he's Deaf because his attitude to him would change. Then Dengel gave some papers to Abel, and the Deaf man signed a contract without reading it. This is why he didn't know about owing monthly payments.

Mr. Dengel is like a hunter whom Abel falls prey to. "Sometimes the man came out and took someone by the arm and smiled to him to come and sit behind the wheel and notice this thing or that, try the horn, try the lights.

Once, Abel was that person." The car salesman was buttering Abel up to convince him to buy the car. Moreover, Dengel talked with a cigar in his mouth that didn't allow Abel to read his lips. I wonder how Dengel couldn't notice something was wrong with Abel while he was talking on and on. The nodding without saying any word a long time should have seemed suspicious. I think Dengel is just self-interested. He, as any businessman, needs money. His main interest was to sell cars, so he didn't care if the customer understood.

I think this trouble would not happen to Abel today because the present time is more civilized. Now Deaf people's lives are different than before when Deaf people always were ashamed of being Deaf and not feeling equal to hearing people. In the future, Abel should let Dengel know beforehand that he is Deaf and ask him to write what he is going to say or ask him politely to take out the cigar from his mouth and try to move his lips clearly. It's hard to guess about Dengel's behavior. In my life, I have never experienced an occasion with an unscrupulous salesperson. I think that a Dengel today would act properly if he is aware that a customer is Deaf. At first, he would ask Abel if he can read lips. If he cannot do that, then, the salesman certainly will write.

Conflict Between Immigrant Parents and Their Children
by Olga

In "An American Dream" by Rosemarie Santini and "The Struggle to Be an All-American Girl" by Elizabeth Wong, we see a conflict of values between younger and older generations. In both stories, the children of immigrant parents prefer American culture and tradition and do not follow their family's tradition. I will offer some reasons for their feelings.

"Where are the children?" asks Grandmother Ida Rinaldi. Grandmother Ida cooked a special dinner to feed her family. She expects them to be together because this is her cultural tradition. However, her grandchildren, John and Paul DeGiovanni, were not at home even though they knew that their family was waiting for them for dinner. John and Paul were busy at the DeGiovanni beach club, swimming and getting ready for a party. They preferred to hang out with their friends and not to be home with their family. "We . . . respected our parents and our family" said Ida's husband Mr. Rinaldi. In addition, he said, "we worked hard." His grandchildren will go to college without having to work; they have everything that they need. They were not the same as he was as a hard-working teenager.

Other conflict between immigrant parents and their children appeared in "The Struggle to be an All-American Girl" by Elizabeth Wong. Elizabeth's mother forced her children to learn and to respect Chinese traditions even though they did not want to. "In Chinese school the children learned mainly language, reading, and writing. The lessons always began with an exercise in politeness." The students in

Chinese school had to learn to be polite and always respect elderly people. They learned Chinese languages by heart. Elizabeth's mother wanted her children to learn to speak Chinese because in Chinatown there were many Chinese people who speak Chinese. She wanted Elizabeth to be able to speak with these people, celebrate Chinese holidays, and eat Chinese food. But Elizabeth did not like the Chinese language because of the loud voice people used with it. Moreover, Elizabeth said, "Nancy Drew, my favorite book heroine, never spoke Chinese."

In my opinion, John and Paul will not resolve the problem with their grandparents. They are not children anymore who need fixing to follow old traditions. They already chose and will hold on to more American ways of life. These ways are comfortable for them, and they do not want to be responsible or help their parents and grandparents. I think it is boring for them to stay home with their family. They prefer to have fun and hang out. Elizabeth and her brother were unhappy with their Chinese school, and it was so hard for them to learn Chinese traditions. Their souls and traditions are now American, and they will not follow Chinese traditions. Elizabeth spoke English in Chinatown even though she knew Chinese. It means forcing her to speak Chinese will be hopeless, and she will not obey what her mother wants. The children of immigrant families in America will choose their own preferred style and culture without their parents' approval. American schools and other teens will influence these children, and it will be hard to teach or explain deeply to them about their own culture and traditions. Their parents have to accept this because they made their children live in America.

References

Anderson, Donald G. 1997. *New Practice Readers, Book B.* 3rd ed. New York: Phoenix Learning Resources.

Anderson, Donald G., Clarence Stone, and Ardis Edwards Burton. 1997. *New Practice Readers, Book A.* 3rd ed. New York: Phoenix Learning Resources.

Baldwin, James. 2004. "The King and the Bees." In *Fifty Famous People* by James Baldwin. Retrieved on June 25, 2010 from www.gutenberg.org/etext/6168.

———. 2004. "The Landlord's Mistake." In *Fifty Famous People* by James Baldwin. Retrieved on June 25, 2010 from www.gutenberg.org/etext/6168.

———. 2004. "The Midnight Ride." In *Fifty Famous People* by James Baldwin. Retrieved on June 25, 2010 from www.gutenberg.org/etext/6168.

———. 2004. "The Paddle-Wheel Boat." In *Fifty Famous People* by James Baldwin. Retrieved on June 25, 2010 from www.gutenberg.org/etext/6168.

———. 2004. "Saving the Birds." In *Fifty Famous People* by James Baldwin. Retrieved on June 25, 2010 from www.gutenberg.org/etext/6168.

———. 2004. "The Story of a Great Story." In *Fifty Famous People* by James Baldwin. Retrieved on June 25, 2010 from www.gutenberg.org/etext/6168.

———. 2004. "Two Great Painters." In *Fifty Famous People* by James Baldwin. Retrieved on June 25, 2010 from www.gutenberg.org/etext/6168.

———. 2004. "Which Was the King?" In *Fifty Famous People* by James Baldwin. Retrieved on June 25, 2010 from www.gutenberg.org/etext/6168.

Baum, L. Frank. 2003. "The Glass Dog." In *American Fairy Tales* by L. Frank Baum. Retrieved on June 25, 2010 from http://www.gutenberg.org/files/4357/4357-h/4357-h.htm.

Blachowicz, Camille L. Z., ed. 2004. *Reading Fluency, Level C.* New York: Glencoe.

Blachowicz, Camille L. Z., ed. 2004. *Reading Fluency, Level D.* New York: Glencoe.

Burningham, John. 1993. *Harvey Slumfenburger's Christmas Present.* Cambridge, MA: Candlewick Press.

Canfield, Jack, Mark Victor Hanson, and Kimberly Kirberger, eds. 1997. *Chicken Soup for the Teenage Soul.* Deerfield Beach, FL: Health Communications.

Cole, Joanna, and Bruce Degen. 1986. *The Magic School Bus at the Waterworks.* New York: Scholastic.

———. 1989. *The Magic School Bus Inside the Human Body.* New York: Scholastic.

Curtis, Jamie Lee. 1993. *When I Was Little.* New York: HarperCollins.

de Maupassant, Guy. 1907. "The Necklace." In *The Short-Story: Specimens Illustrating Its Development*, ed. Brander Matthews. New York: American Book Company. Retrieved on July 15, 2007, from www.bartleby.com/195/20.html.

De Young, C. Coco. 1999. *A Letter to Mrs. Roosevelt.* New York: Random House.

Dorros, Arthur. 1987. *Ant Cities.* New York: HarperCollins.

Duncan, Lois. 1990. *Killing Mr. Griffin.* New York: Random House.

Inturrisi, Louis. 1980. *The Ways of Written English.* New York: Language Innovations, Inc.

Jiang, Ji Li. 1997. *Red Scarf Girl: A Memoir of the Cultural Revolution.* New York: HarperCollins.

Kunz, Linda, and Laurie Gluck. 2000. "X-Word Grammar Intermediate." The English Language Center, LaGuardia Community College, The City University of New York.

L'Hommedieu, John. 1997. *From Plant to Blue Jeans.* New York: Children's Press.

Lowry, Lois. 2004. "Splendor." In *Reading Fluency*, ed. Camille L. Z. Blachowicz, 29. New York: Glencoe.

Nickle, John. 1999. *The Ant Bully.* New York: Scholastic.

Paterson, Katherine. 1979. "Angels and Other Strangers." In *A Christmas Treasury*, 57–74. New York: Scholastic.

Reading for Concepts, Book A. 3rd ed. 1999. New York: Phoenix Learning Resources.

Robnoxious. 2003. "The Year Is 1902." Retrieved on January 10, 2003, from www.goofball.com/jokes/facts/2003016101.

Rylant, Cynthia. 1982. *When I Was Young in the Mountains.* New York: Puffin Unicorn.

———. 1998. *The Bird House.* New York: Scholastic.

Sachar, Louis. 1989. *Wayside School Is Falling Down.* New York: Avon Books.

Seuling, Barbara. 2000. *Drip! Drop! How Water Gets to Your Tap.* New York: Holiday House.

Voigt, Cynthia. 1981. *Homecoming.* New York: Fawcett Juniper.

White, E. B. 1952. *Charlotte's Web.* New York: Harper & Row.